I0416694

FRIENDS TO DIE FOR

By

Rosalind W. Johnson

This book is a work of fiction. Places, events, and situations in this story are purely fictional. Any resemblance to actual persons, living or dead, is coincidental.

© 2003 by Rosalind W. Johnson. All rights reserved.

No part of this book may be reproduced, stored in a retrieval system, or transmitted by any means, electronic, mechanical, photocopying, recording, or otherwise, without written permission from the author.

ISBN: 1-4107-1145-5 (e-book)
ISBN: 1-4107-1146-3 (Paperback)

Library of Congress Control Number: 2003090078

This book is printed on acid free paper.

Printed in the United States of America
Bloomington, IN

1stBooks – rev. 02/13/04

MAY

Well pretty girl, what would your parents and Aunt Heleena say if they could see you now? Turning from the window, his hard eyes swept the beautiful girl sleeping naked between the twisted sheets and pillows. A fine sheen of moisture covered her body.

Moving to the bed he began stroking the springy bronze strands curling down her back, his thoughts unconnected to the loving gesture. *You are perfect, just the person I need. Even a fortnight of Grandma Tina's prayers is no match for the God who sent you to me.*

Though always tender, loving her long and slow, his eyes were now cold and calculating. His mouth, just hours before, the sensual instrument sending life and hope through every corner of her body; now set hard as stone. The plans he'd made for her were not those of a lover, but of a skillful and cunning manipulator. But she had no experience to alert her to his duplicitous nature. She could not know that his soul didn't extend to those hands that touched lightly as a feather.

Before returning to the window, he placed a warm kiss on her slender neck. Judy moaned in her sleep, secure in his touch, but the lover's kiss carried the sting of death.

Chapter 1

"Twenty three, twenty four, twenty five," she counted, glancing at the clock on the table. "Fifteen more minutes."

Her daily work-out consisted of forty sit-ups and an equal number of leg lifts and arm curls. Even as the phone rang for the second time this morning, she refused to answer it. "Just Karen trying to ruin the start of my day with Judy's problems. If she can't stop her headlong rush into self-destruction, neither can I. Every one of us has lived with a broken heart. Loving the wrong man never killed any woman."

As she counted each move, there was no way she could know that the shadow of death waited just around the corner and by the end of summer their lives would be turned upside down. Then she'd long for the insistent ring of the phone and the voice of her friend at the other end.

"Thirty seven, thirty eight, thirty nine... Between Karen dumping on me about her children and Marva about her husband, neither one of them cares that I could use a little TLC myself right now."

Forty-six years old, beautiful, successful in every way, but now restlessness settled on her with a vengeance. These stirrings begged for something new, another chance to choose, leave Roosevelt, buy a smaller house, begin serious dating again.

While working intolerable hours, Heleena had given all of the remaining time to her children. Johnny was now in graduate school and Richie with his dad. Greg decided she babied him too much. Anne remained in Atlanta for the summer, living in the same apartment they'd rented for her at the beginning of her sophomore year. She had blocks of empty hours now, time to sort through unresolved issues.

Greg left her to live with a woman he met at a convention. His only explanation after twelve years of marriage was the marriage had been a mistake. He was right.

She met him through Karen and Scooter. Karen arranged blind dates for her and Marva with Scooter's best friends, Al Harris and Greg Walton, two good looking interns. Blind dates are always chancy; I should have been on guard.

Marva didn't know either of them, but Heleena had met Al on two previous occasions. It was natural for her to believe he would be her date, but it didn't happen that way.

Half a lifetime later, Heleena still felt Marva was the lucky one. She, on the other hand, married the ringer and often wondered where her life might have gone had she been Al's date that night. In spite of everything, they remained the closest friends, always enjoying life together as a tight unit.

Those early years were an exciting time in their young lives. They were invincible, living life on their own terms. At what point did it start to come apart? That was the question she'd asked herself in the middle of many a lonely night. What happened?

* * *

The physical difference between these two was obvious, the personality differences not so noticeable. Two handsome people. Al, 6'4", was still lean at 53 years of age. Marva 5'2" and five years younger, was always described as cute because of her doll-like face and pixie hairdo.

They'd been together almost twenty-six years and appeared compatible. Each had learned to flow with the other's rhythm, but as they moved around the expansive kitchen this bright Friday morning, less obvious was how each accepted the new day. Al was a morning person, unlike Marva who stayed in bed until the last possible moment. Today, however, she rose early, trying to cool her husband's anger at their daughter's late nights with her new boyfriend. He'd been up since 5:00 a.m.

"Why was Selena out until 3:00 a.m.? What was she doing and where was she?"

"Whoa--One question at a time."

"What's going on with her? This isn't the first time."

"She's in love. You remember love don't you?"

He refused to be drawn into another argument with her, so made no comment.

"She's dating that guy she met in Atlanta."

"He's from Atlanta?"

"No. Philadelphia is his home, but he lives here now."

"Where?"

"Out in Prince George's County somewhere." His annoying questions plucked every one of her nerves. "Is there something wrong Al?"

"Nothing's wrong with her dating, but staying out until all hours in the morning? What is she doing?"

"The exact same thing you and I did when we were dating. Remember?"

"I want her in this house earlier than two or three in the morning."

"For God's sake she is a grown woman. She doesn't have to kowtow to everything we, no make that, everything you want."

"I'm not concerned with having her do everything my way, it's just that I don't want her hanging out in the streets until all hours of the morning."

"Then you tell her."

"I will."

"Al, sometimes I think you forget what it's like to be young and in love. Do you ever remember what it was like for us?" She turned around and looked at him with hope in her eyes.

3

He peered over his glasses, his eyes piercing her to the core, "Since you are bent on remembering this morning, do you recall we did not have a protracted courtship."

"True," she agreed, "but we were young and carefree."

"Marva, please don't pull against me in this. Selena is vulnerable. I want you to help me persuade her to go slowly with this relationship. I don't want her hurt again."

"Neither do I. But, she has to make her own decisions."

There was little warmth in Al's voice when he replied, "You're her mother, don't you want to see her profit from the mistakes we made, and to use your phrase, when we were young?"

"What I want is for her to have a full rich life; one where she can love and have love in return. Only she can make that choice; not me, not you, or anyone else can pick a man for her."

"I'm not trying to pick a man for her. I'm worried because the hurt left when Calvin walked out on her, is still raw."

Marva sat down at the table across from him as he made notes in patient charts. The self-assured manner in which he ran his life never changed in all the years she'd known him; the twenty-five years of their marriage and the five months preceding their hastily arranged wedding.

I am still amazed he agreed to marry me.

She rarely let herself dwell on her determined capture of such a prize. Al always seemed to have his way in this world. Everything worked for him. He organized his life on his own terms. He methodically built a thriving and successful medical practice. No one who knew him could fail to understand why he bore the nickname, Prince; tall, eyes, deep clear pools, never wavering. His coloring, a rich burnished brown, like fine pecan wood, and sculptured lips always ready to charm. Shimmering gray flecks gave him an air of distinction and power.

This morning he wore an eggshell-colored polo, opened at the neck. As she sat looking at him her heart soared once again; the feeling just as intense as the first time she ever saw him. As though she willed him to, he looked up over his glasses. For three seconds their eyes locked and held. What she saw in his had nothing to do with their daughter. It was a mirror of the old accusation, "You did not play fair with me." Lowering his eyes Al continued writing.

But she wanted his attention. "What do you want me to do with Selena, give her an ultimatum?"

"I just want you to support me, okay?"

They'd given Selena much more leeway during her teens than Heleena and their other friends gave their children. Now Al wanted to put the skids on her. "I'll talk to her when I get home."

She was reluctant to end these few moments with him. Lately time together was rare, so she searched furiously for a subject to keep his attention.

He sensed there was something else she wanted to say, she kept fidgeting in her chair. "Go on, say what's on your mind."

"It's been a long time since we shared a domestic scene like this. All the ideas that run through my mind during the day are lost by the time you get home at night. If it weren't for Selena's love life we wouldn't be here talking together this morning."

His lips parted in that heart-stopping smile. "Sweetheart, you're usually sleeping late, with just minutes to dress, before running out of the house. There is absolutely nothing I can do about working long hours, but if you want to talk to me about anything we can talk just as we're doing now or you can come by the office, or wait until I get home."

"Do I need to make an appointment with you, like one of your patients?"

"Marva, for God's sake, both of us are busy. Whatever it is you want to talk to me about, I'll take an entire afternoon away from the office so you can get it off your chest. Jay will see my patients."

"You don't understand." She needed to pick her words carefully. The last thing she wanted was another argument with him. "I don't have anything specific to discuss with you. I'm simply commenting that being here, together, in the morning, like married couples all over the world, is something we don't do anymore."

Her frustration was rising, but with great effort she smothered the feeling and tried again. "Do you have any plans for this weekend?"

"No. I thought you, Selena, and I might have dinner out tomorrow night."

She was so surprised she stammered, "Where?"

"Any place you want. You like seafood. Why not Pinder's in Georgetown. They have excellent shrimp and lobster."

"Oh, Al, that's a great place. We haven't been there in ages, not since your mother was here."

"We're on then."

A small ray of hope bloomed inside her. Maybe things will be better between us. Al is a fine man and a good husband -- well, in comparison with many others I know. If only we had the kind of relationship I envisioned when he married me. I have his name, sleep in his bed, have the same rights wives have everywhere, but his core; that part of him that makes him who he is, still eludes me.

Sipping her coffee she thought back to their first date. Al and Greg, two of Scooter's friends, I was ready and willing.

"Be good to these guys," Karen admonished them. "They're the best."

Right away Heleena tried to stake a claim. "I met Al at a wedding, took my breath away, he is so fine."

"And Greg is just as fine," Karen said. "If you play your cards right, both of you will do as good as I did. Heleena you know Al is a serious catch."

"I thought you said both of them were good catches."

"They are."

"What did you tell them about us?" Heleena wanted to know.

"Nothing much, only you were two gorgeous girls who just happened to be available."

"Available for what?" Heleena asked.

"Available for dates. What else? Remember now, this is your golden opportunity. Girls are chasing them ferociously, especially Al. He's been in the military, so he's probably ready to settle down, don't you think so Heleena?"

"All I can say is he seems like a dream. But I want to know what they are expecting. A quick lay?"

"No, but, I don't know any man who isn't looking for the real deal."

My only thought that night was, no problem. Right then I decided what I was going to do. It sounded like Al was ripe. He was mine.

"Everything will work out. I knew I had Scooter hooked, the minute he walked in here, that first night."

"And he couldn't believe his good fortune. The ironic thing is poor Scooter didn't know he held the winning ticket."

"He was the winning ticket."

The three of them burst into laughter. They knew the story backwards.

When the doorbell rang, Karen jumped from the bed.

"Be cool now. Be cool," she said walking toward the door.

When she opened the door, there they stood, two tall men, movie-star handsome, with inviting smiles. Greg stood a little to the front of Al. Heleena smiled back, her eyes on Al, but I made my move the minute he crossed the threshold. He was everything Karen had said and more. I knew I would do anything to have him as my very own, but what happened to the excitement and enthusiasm of that night?

She looked at her gold watch and sighed, "I might as well dress and get out of here."

"You sound like you're going off somewhere to be punished."

"Exactly. I'm sick of that place. All day we do nothing but push paper. I don't know how much longer I can go down there."

"You don't have to stay in that job. I've told you before to leave if you're so miserable."

"I'm thinking about doing just that, believe me."

* * *

Al is always good to me, has been right from the beginning. He has never said a mean thing to me. I just wish I had his heart. She stopped fastening her blouse and set on the bench in front of the mirror. Fear of losing him, which she'd ignored in the past, visited her more and more these days -- sometimes as a knot in her chest, other times, an angry curve in the pit of her stomach.

He married me, she consoled herself, while making a valiant effort at keeping the doubts and fears at bay.

Hearing his determined steps on the stairs she quickly pulled herself together. By the time he came through the door she'd slipped on her three-inch heels and reached for her jacket.

"Marva, I plan to call Mama today. I want to coordinate her visit with Theresa's. Have you decided when you're going back to Tuskegee?"

"In three weeks. I wanted to wait until after the dance, but Alva will be home then and we thought it would be nice if both of us were there at the same time. We haven't been home together since we buried Daddy."

"Why don't you have her come up here and stay for a while, maybe during Mama's visit. They get along well together."

Just what I need, two more women in this house. "I'll try, but you know how she likes to be involved in everything that happens in her church. They're looking for a new pastor, so she's very active right now."

"Ask her anyway. It's been too long since her last visit."

He started toward the dressing room, but turned and came back to where she stood. Placing a hand on both cheeks he turned her face upward, "Remember, you don't have to work. If you're unhappy, leave."

She blinked several times, breaking the spell. For a minute I thought you were going to kiss me.

"Promise me?"

"I'll give it serious thought, thanks."

He was through the door of the dressing room in an instant. Fool, she scolded herself. He is good to all the women in his life. Of course he cares about you, and Selena, Heleena, his mama. So don't hear something more in his words than the concern that is a natural part of him. Take whatever he gives you girl. Get off this bed and straighten your face, he belongs to you.

Somehow that assurance did not do much to lift her spirits.

She'd attributed the tension she felt between her and Al, to this time in her life. That was her hope anyway.

"Al. Al," she called.

"Hum?"

"I forgot to tell you, Carl called about the dance. Apparently the tickets are going fast, do you want a table or are you sitting at Karen and Scooter's table?"

"We're sitting with them. I'll call him later, after I talk to Heleena. She may want to invite someone."

She walked to the door and stood where she could see him. "I don't think so. When is the last time she invited anybody? Can you remember?"

"No, but she may have someone in mind."

"Have you talked to her lately?"

"Why?"

"She's feeling down. I noticed a change since she returned from that reunion. I think she wants a man."

Al walked back through to the dressing room. "What did you say?"

"Heleena is feeling the need for a man, but she's discovering they're hard to find."

"Did she say that to you?"

"Uh, Huh. When she went back to her reunion, there were so many divorced women there, in her own words, she almost gagged."

"You're exaggerating."

"No I'm not. She probably hasn't mentioned it to you yet because she hasn't seen you since she returned."

"I told her she certainly doesn't have to concern herself with that bull." He went back into the other room and she followed him.

"Will you be home for dinner?"

"I should be here around seven. You make sure Selena knows I want to talk to her, tonight."

She bristled and made her way to her dressing room. Inside, among the dresses, shoes and bags, she fought for calm. Marva, he is only trying to protect her. What about me, she argued with herself. He married you. He gives you everything. No. Not everything. Be honest, he gave you just what you wanted from him, that piece of paper declaring the two of you one. And he does want your happiness. I don't know that. She continued the personal debate. You should.

Back in the bedroom, she resumed her seat on the bench. Al set at the French desk talking on the phone. She grabbed her purse and left the room.

An hour later she leaned forward, her chin resting in her hands. There is not a woman alive who would have risked loosing him. I still have no regrets. He loves his daughter, always has, right from the day she was born, but it's not right after all these years, I should still be waiting for his whole love. It's wearing me thin.

* * *

By the time the powerful black sports car roared into the parking lot, Mrs. Hawkins was ready with everything Al needed to begin his

9

day. She originally came to work for him as part-time help, twenty-four years ago. She never thought to stay, but they'd made a smooth team.

For the first two years it had been just the two of them. Then came Medicaid and all hell broke loose. They hired one other person, then another until soon there were seven people bumping into each other. He expanded into the extra space available.

At eleven he sat behind his desk sipping a cup of coffee. "Mrs. Hawkins get Heleena on the phone please and remind me to call Carl around noon. I need to talk to her first."

She knew where to reach Ms. Walton this time of the morning. To the doctor and his wife she was family.

"Ms. Walton I have Dr. Harris on the line."

"Hey sweetheart. How are you?"

"Fine."

"So, what else is new? Listen, I just want to make sure you're coming with us to the scholarship dance."

"Yes, why?"

"Marva thought you were having a problem coming without an escort." Before she could answer he continued, "You're not worried about that are you?"

"Well -- maybe."

"Look, how many times must I assure you, you'll never want for a good time when you're with us.

"I know you mean that, but sometimes I want an escort of my own."

"Do you have someone in mind?"

"That's a laugh. Who?"

"It's settled then."

"I guess." She was silent for a minute. "You always manage to jerk me back to reality."

"I'll talk to you later, but I wanted to make sure you weren't pulling out."

Within minutes he was back with his patients. The time he spent in his work was the most satisfying. Even so, his wife thought he spent too much time in the office.

By the end of the day he was drained. He didn't need Marva or Mrs. Hawkins to remind him he was seeing more patients, reversing the trend of recent years.

Finally alone, he went up to the small apartment on the top floor, hoping to relax quietly before heading home.

On the sofa, one long leg stretched over the cushions; he lay back with his eyes closed. *Why do I have doubts now and this burning need to keep busy?*

The arguments with my baby, are they about me? Am I looking at my own young life? Can I even help her see how important it is for her to take her time with this relationship? Love is not always what it appears to be. What is so clear today can break her heart down the road.

Agitated, he went to the kitchen and mixed a gin and tonic. Back in the living room, he put on an old Bobby Blue Bland tune and smiled at the irony of the words coming out at him.

Rosalind W. Johnson

Chapter 2

The two men sitting around the table in the dark room were enveloped in a haze of sickly, sweet-smelling smoke. "We get them to go and bring package back on weekend. That way we have time to prepare by Monday night." Peter's accent was thick tonight.

The second man did not answer, only nodded his head in agreement.

"This time we send somebody different. Sheila no more. She made three trips already. That's enough."

"Who?"

The long dread locks touched the table as he moved his head closer to his companion and whispered, "My woman, Judy."

"Judy?"

"Shish," Peter whispered, anger contorting his features.

"Why?"

"This is special run *mon*, important. No old faces. Why you think I call only you. No one must know. If I send anybody else, is big trouble. This deal is family."

Ansel knew what he meant. They were cousins, raised in the same house, their mothers, sisters. When Peter's father sent for him to come to New York, Ansel's mother sent him too. The only time they lived apart was the year Peter went to college. A bright student, he entered Howard University with a full scholarship, but learned more in that one year than most students learn during their entire four years. Peter had a natural gift of persuasion. Not only did he exhibit winning ways with the opposite sex, he was smooth in getting others to do his bidding.

Sometime during that year the lure of the streets emerged stronger than the classroom. Hanging out with the natives of the city, he started with plain old fashioned pimping, honing his skills. With his smarts and good looks he ran a thriving business. Then boredom set in and he needed more excitement in his entrepreneurial endeavors, so he began running his girls to Richmond and Wilmington. The money came easily. By March of that school year he stopped attending classes altogether, and leaped into the big time.

Quickly discovering how to traffic in another more valuable commodity, he opened his own pipeline and began his career in the booming Washington drug market. Beginning with marijuana he soon escalated to cocaine, then to an even more deadly substance, the little white rocks known as crack. Next, came the .9mm guns. He sent for the ever-faithful Ansel and higher education was no longer an option.

Before the end of what would have been his second year of college, Peter had created a drug pipeline extending from Dunn's River Falls to New York City. He cleverly used his extraordinary good looks in recruiting women as pawns in his dangerous enterprise. Lonely disaffected American girls were easy prey. Washington, DC was full of pretty, young girls, middle class girls whose parents had sent them off to school with all their hopes and dreams. For a man like Peter they were fish bait.

* * *

A highway of dreams, I-95 had been bringing people from Florida to DC, Philadelphia and New York for decades. It was still the most efficient conduit for making the long journey along the east coast. Only now a new and terrifying traveler was on the venerable old highway, purveyors transporting illegal drugs destined for New York and other points in the Northeast.

Some of the smarter boys, however, used detours. Many of them now took to the back roads, two-lane state highways, through small southern towns. Of course that only worked when they paid the local law authority. Times had changed but Jim Crow still sat on his throne and reigned supreme from North Florida, through the dusty towns of Georgia, North Carolina and Virginia. He sat by the side of the road, unbowed, unblemished, and totally without apology.

The local law in the picturesque little town of Dover in Tenneco County, South Carolina, was Sheriff Tommy Lee McHickey, who worshipped at the feet of Ole Jim. To describe his love of Jim as adoration is to put it mildly. His love approached messianic fervor.

Tommy Lee stood tall in his community, attended church every Sunday, spent time with his wife, and even her ailing mother. He could do all of these things, you see, because there was little crime in Dover. Oh, he knew about the contraband passing through neighboring towns, but no one had ever approached him to offer compensation for the use of Tenneco roads. They knew better, for Tommy Lee was a God-faring man, unforgiving of drug pushers. The citizens of Dover did not know about his activities relating to the disappearance of the two black migrants passing through who were never heard from again. No, they did not know about that.

* * *

Peter cleverly drew others to his bidding. He was cunning, never openly challenging the people who supplied him. His guest did not look much like an emissary of death, but Peter, knew better. This man traveled the globe dispensing every man's vice.

"This is the plan *mon*. Judy will fly down and stay with Bruce and Christie, two weeks. Christie will send someone to drive back with her."

"How do you know she can handle this job?" He asked, his voice cultured and British.

Never one to apologize for his decisions, giving orders suited Peter and explanations only as he thought necessary. This man, however, was his key to mega dividends, so it was in his best interest to convince him of the soundness of the plan.

"She's a natural. I brought her into another deal and she performed well." He lied. Judy trusted him without question and believed whatever he said to her. Whether she knew his business, did not matter, she was trusting and pliable.

His eyes shone with the intensity of a person who knew with certainty that his plan was without fault. "Leave her to me *mon*." He wasn't able to stop himself from slipping into his heavy island accent.

This trip involved three times the usual amount of merchandise. He wanted to stick to the transport methods he'd used before, but those who gave the orders thought it wise to use new routes, with prudence of course.

Peter wanted more opportunities. This deal was his answer. If anything went wrong, he knew he'd pay the awful price. So he had no compunction about using anyone to effectuate his success. He spread the map across the table and the two of them leaned over squinting in the bright light of the arc lamp as he pointed out the route the travelers would take. Using a long finger, Peter started at the tip of the marshy coast of Florida moving slowly north following the red line of Interstate 95. It was a perfect route with all the little picturesque beach towns along the way; Delray Beach, Jupiter, Stuart, Fort Pierce, Vero Beach, and Daytona. They were places that saw tourists come and go year round.

"Two women with children driving a ten-year old station wagon will not draw attention."

"What about the tags?"

"Legitimate and legal. I sent the car down there three weeks ago." The man seemed satisfied with the answer. Peter continued, "They will sleep the night in Jacksonville. I don't want them tiring on the road and having to sleep in the car at some rest park or truck stop." He looked up to see if there were any questions. His guest remained silent.

"Outside Jacksonville they switch to US 1, right into Georgia." His finger continued moving along the eastern edge of the great Okefenokee Swamp. "They will remain on US 1 until just beyond the intersection with US 20 near Ft. Gordon. About 30 minutes later they will reach Highway 78. There they will take 78 into South Carolina." Both of them leaned forward, heads almost touching as their eyes fixed on this small dot of a place.

"In Greenwood they take 72 to US 77 North to Interstate 85." Peter's finger moved slowly past the small mill towns that dotted this stretch of roads through South Carolina. Inconspicuously displayed on the map, was little Dover.

As they studied the map and surrounding areas, the visitor could find no fault with the chosen route. The final part of the trip put them just south of Richmond where US 85 ran into I-95. They would stay on 95 into Maryland.

"My concern is the two women. What do they know?"

Peter was careful to keep irritation out of his voice. This was his operation and he did not like being questioned about it. He'd planned meticulously, justifying every aspect of the trip.

He looked straight at his visitor, eyes unwavering. "I send my woman to Miami to meet my aunts. All she knows is that she will drive back with my cousin's wife and his two children. She does not know anything about the merchandise concealed in the car." His tone of voice challenged his guest to find fault with the plan.

There was one thing this man did not like, but he said nothing. It was Peter himself. From all their investigation of him, they could not find what factors motivated him. He lived in a God-forsaken jungle in Baltimore with none of the trappings these boys usually attached to themselves. He was smart and planned like a military general. Too smart, maybe.

"Tell me about these girls."

"They do what I tell them to do, no questions asked. It is nothing for you to worry about."

"I worry about everything. If the people you and I work for, don't get their merchandise I am dead and so are you. When I report back on this deal and the people involved, I need to tell them even about the mules."

Peter pushed his chair back from the table and carefully stood. He walked to the only window in the room, using the few seconds to compose himself. Calmed, he faced his guest.

"Judy will go to Miami alone. I promised her a visit to meet my relatives. She expects to marry me by year's end. This visit will be her first and she is anxious and compliant. She's been told that my cousin's woman needs help driving his car up from Florida. The timing is perfect."

17

The man pressed on, "Is this promise of marriage for real or a ploy?"

With Herculean effort he responded calmly, "I do what I need to do. A promise of marriage or marriage itself is part of my plans. You needn't worry, there are no personal feelings to get in the way. She's expendable."

His visitor knew he meant every word. He'd seen men like Peter all over the world, charismatic and confidant of their own abilities. They had no feelings and used women for the riskiest jobs, priming them with words of love. More often than not these were the most successful in the business. Yes, he thought, the plan seemed workable, but he needed to stay on top of everything, right up to its execution.

"I will get back to you before the girls leave Miami." Saying nothing further, he walked out, closing the door softly.

Seething, Peter set at the table, not moving, for over an hour. "Who are these people?" He'd carefully planned his operation and needed a special type of girl. Judy turned out to be the perfect choice; lonely, gullible, and needing love. Her emotional estrangement from her family was a bonus. No problem with her.

* * *

When she came to him later her longing glowed in her eyes. There were no doubts about his feelings toward her. Like all Casanovas, he had a way with women, the way he touched her when talking or running his fingers through her hair. She really wasn't hard to love.

Judy Topley, born May 4, 1978, a second child, destined forever to be not quite as good. She was beautiful, more striking than her mother. Her coloring, a blend of both parents, a mite darker than Karen wanted, but not too dark. A sweet, quiet child, never asserting herself, always looking for approval. She'd had crushes on boys, like any young girl. Somehow they never measured up to family standards and always ended abruptly. Until college. Finally she was in a place protected from the microscopic scrutiny of her parents, but she was green, inexperienced, and easy prey.

He wrapped her in his arms, "Can you stay tonight?" The asking was part of his seductive web. It meant nothing, for she never denied him anything.   He knew this but was careful and never took advantage of her feelings.

Before answering she pressed her lips to his, wanting the feel of him, needing him. "Can I?" The question was a child's hope.

Caressing her back and nicely rounded behind, he held her to him, tightly, showing her. The sound of her moans cut short as his lips hardened, demanding more. She wanted nothing but this time with him. She had no need to be anybody else, she only needed to please him. Something she lived every day of her life to do.

Two beautiful people. When morning found them the sun was high and the heat already oppressive in the tiny room. Uncovered, they lay together on the bed, beads of perspiration covering their beautiful bodies. She buried her face in the nape of his neck with her hair spread over his back. Turning over, he gathered her to him, loving her one more time. She didn't bother thinking about anything or anybody else; this was her life.

Rosalind W. Johnson

Chapter 3

"What did the girls say about your new bracelet?"

"They were cool when I showed it to them."

"What?"

"Sometimes those bitches are distant, to me anyway.

Billie was her usual catty self. All she said was 'Not everybody can walk around with a two-carat diamond bracelet on her arm.' Of course I had to tell the stupid bitch it was five carats. They're mostly Heleena's friends and I always felt they were just jealous of me."

"People are like that honey. Don't let their meanness get next to you."

"I tell myself that all the time but I know how they feel."

"How was Heleena's trip?"

"That's all they talked about. They kept teasing her because apparently seeing all her old classmates made her feel she's missed something. Heleena of all people, can you believe that?"

"Missed what?"

"Hearth and home."

21

Scooter looked at her in disbelief, "You mean back down South?"

"No, husband and all that goes with the deal." Karen waved a hand through the air for emphasis.

Showing a mouth full of brilliant white teeth, he laughed. "I know she can't possibly miss Greg after all this time."

"No, Not Greg, just marriage and having somebody."

"Who?"

"Nobody in particular. I think she is just feeling sorry for herself. A couple of weeks ago she said something odd. I didn't pay any attention at the time, but now I believe I understand what she meant. I think our girl wants a man and bad. Any man."

Sunday morning with no plans, they were still upstairs in bed. Scooter braced against the elaborate headboard, remote in hand, watched TV. Karen had the newspaper spread across the bed.

He'd learned to wait for her to propose some mutual activity when they had time together. When the children were growing up they had little spare time, now they could do more of what they were doing, nothing.

I miss my son. Thinking back to the day Junior left home, a flicker of pain crossed his face. The family was already under siege. At night they went to their individual bedrooms, closing the doors. Conversations inevitably turned into arguments. Karen laid down the rules and expected her family to follow them.

Judy had no stomach for challenge. She'd complied with all her mother's rules until she found an outside interest, someone willing to accept her with no requirements to change. Junior, on the other hand, determined to be his own man, even to that last day.

Closing his eyes, he tried to block out the remembered pain of that evening. "I am sick of you looking like Topsy," Karen said for what seemed like the hundredth time.

They were seated around the table in the breakfast room, having supper. Ms. Anderson had gone for the day. Since this was not the first time Karen had said as much to him, he wisely made no response, but she continued.

"Did you hear me?"

He put his fork down and started to push his chair back from the table.

"Don't you hear your mother talking to you?"

"So, she's sick of me. What else is new?"

"It's not you, but that stupid hairdo."

"Stupid?" He was standing now. "Why is the way I wear my hair stupid?"

"Hair twisted into little knots and sticking all around your head looks silly."

He looked at his mother. She was the one responsible for opinions in the family. Out of habit he knew only she could change his father's mind. "Ma, why does everything we do offend you? We don't look right, we don't talk right, we ought not to even exist in your eyes." His voice had risen to a trembling pitch and his eyes watered. "I'm sick and tired of this shit. Judy and I are just fucks gone to waste."

He was out of his chair and gone from the room before they realized it. Karen paled. Scooter's eyes were like round moons. He jumped from his chair and started after his son, but Karen grabbed his arm, holding him back.

Junior left that night and had not been in the house since. He sighed.

"What is that for?" Karen rubbed his stomach.

"I was thinking about Junior. It just slipped out."

"He's okay. If he weren't we'd find out from someone."

"Probably, but I still miss him."

"He is just like your brother, Jerry," she said.

"But things were simpler when he left home. All he had to do was work hard everyday until finally he made something of himself. Junior was raised differently. He didn't have to worry about whether he would eat or if his home would be his home next month or sometimes the next day."

"They're cut from the same cloth is all I'm saying. Have you heard from Jerry lately?"

"No, not for a couple of months. He and Mae were about to leave for their yearly trip to Honolulu."

"Old dumpy Mae. She needs to do something about herself. You would think being married to a successful businessman she'd try to improve her looks and get rid of some of those pounds. It's still a mystery to me what he saw in her."

"She is a wonderful person. You just never got to know her."

"What is there to know? She bows and scrapes and jumps every time Jerry looks her way."

"She's what he's needed all his life, a woman who puts him first."

"It took him long enough. What about wife number one and wife number two?"

"They just didn't work out. It happens every day."

"Give me a break. My advise to Mae is she'd better watch her step. Jerry has an itch in his pants."

He smiled. She was right on target this time. Jerry was a ladies' man, always had been. At sixteen he was a father. Just a few months later, he left town, headed north. Tifton, Georgia was not big enough for him and the baby's family. He'd gone to live with their aunt in Cincinnati.

His parents breathed a sigh of relief, as much because they had one less mouth to feed as to have him away from the baby's family. Twenty years passed before he ever set foot in his home town again.

"What do you want to do today?" He asked.

"Let's call Heleena, see what she's up to."

* * *

The house set on a small rise at the end of a street, heavily wooded with oak and maple trees, mingled with evergreen. Homes in this area were large and set back into their sites guaranteeing the owners' privacy. This wasn't a neighborhood for house-to-house chit chat.

When Scooter and Karen arrived they saw Marva's Jaq parked out front. Once inside they saw Heleena had invited two other couples, Penny and Jeff Goldstein and the Browns, Bill and his wife Fay.

They'd gathered in the loggia between the two wings of the house. Scooter made drinks for Karen and himself then joined the spirited discussion of the civil rights struggle in light of the current political climate: was it dead?

"Heleena, you certainly can't complain; partner in one of the biggest law firms in the country."

"What about the thousands of others who went into those big firms and companies. After years of toiling and selling, many of them now find themselves standing by while young whites move above them. Or worse, being let go on the eve of retirement. They played by the rules, then the rules abruptly changed."

"But they have all the skills they need; education and experience."

"Very few people know how to start over in their forties and fifties."

"See, that is exactly my point. Plants are shutting down, companies downsizing and jobs are being lost everywhere, why is this a black problem?"

"It's not a black problem, but it's a problem that is driving black people nuts."

"I still contend they have nothing to complain about."

"Jeff, it's a good thing I know you mean well."

She was standing behind the bar. Jeff sat on a bar stool opposite her. Penny had edged away from his side and was now sitting between Karen and Marva. Al standing at the end of the bar, moved next to Heleena, put his glass down and leaned over with both arms resting on the edge.

"Jeff, we've known each other, how many years would you say?"

"Twenty years? For as long as I've known Heleena anyway."

"What kind of guy would you call me?"

"The best."

"I'll accept that, but be more specific. Come on, we're friends. We're comfortable. Tell me."

All eyes were now on them.

"You're smart, damn good physician, sure of your place in the world and you have a beautiful wife."

"All that and more," Heleena interjected.

"But, have you ever seen me bitch or whine or blame white boys for anything?"

"Of course not. I wasn't talking about you or anyone here."

"Well, who?"

"Every time I pick up a newspaper, your leaders are blaming the plight of blacks on other people. The time has come for black people to start looking at themselves and what they are or are not doing."

"Be careful of your audience next time you give your opinion about black people. The same problems so prominently discussed in the papers about us are the same problems infecting the rest of America. But no one is anxious to point out the facts to whites who are also falling by the wayside, losing much of the security they've learned to count on for a lifetime."

"He knows better," Heleena said. There was no rancor in her voice. Jeff had served in the heat of battle and he still cared, but his honesty had too sharp an edge and she had said so to him.

"Al, don't misunderstand me. The barriers which held your people back for generations are gone. You must look at other reasons for problems plaguing the people."

"You're one of the few whites I'd stand to say to me what you've just said."

Palms up, Jeff spread his hands. "I just think it's something that ought to be discussed."

"By us," Al insisted. "Don't get too comfortable with your analogy of our problems. No matter how much you want to help, you can never know what it means to see the world from a face the color of mine."

Heleena squeezed his arm. This conversation was getting too heated for a relaxing Sunday afternoon. Al was holding back on his rising displeasure with Jeff's statements. She could detect the soft southern brogue creeping into his voice.

She moved behind him carrying a pitcher in one hand and a bag of tortilla chips in the other and squeezed onto the couch next to Penny.

"Is my husband at it again?"

"I'm afraid so."

"You know he doesn't mean any harm."

"If I weren't sure of that, our friendship would have been short lived. But, Al won't let talk like that go over his head."

Out of one ear Heleena could hear the hum of continued conversation between Al, Jeff and now Scooter. She did, however, notice the decrease in the intensity of their voices.

"Come and help me set out the food," Heleena said to the women as she stood to leave the room. Immediately, Marva began to set the table in a corner bay between the kitchen and family room.

"How far would you go in disagreeing with your husband?" Fay directed her question to Karen, who was closest to her.

"As far as it takes for him to come around to my way of seeing things."

"Ain't that the truth," Marva agreed, rolling her eyes.

"Seriously?" Fay insisted.

"I am serious. My husband seldom disagrees with me."

Marva walked over to Karen and Fay. "Scooter's only desire in life is to please this woman."

"And he pays for it every day of his life," Heleena added jokingly.

"Her husband worships her. We should be so lucky," Marva added.

"My husband is good to me." Holding out her left arm the glittering diamond bracelet sparkled outrageously. "This is his latest goody."

"Wow, that is gorgeous." Fay pulled her wrist closer, admiring the beautiful piece. "What was the occasion?"

"Just that he loves me."

"What she's trying to tell you is that Scooter sees everything from her point of view."

"Well," Fay said, this time directing her question to Marva. "How strongly do you disagree with Al?"

"Only for as long as I can hold his attention."

"Out with it Fay," Heleena said. "What is it you want to say to us?"

She hesitated, but started anyway. "Being married to a black man and coming from a different background, isn't always easy."

"Correction," Marva interjected. "Marriage to a black man period, isn't easy, but go on with your point."

"Bill always had definite ideas about the children, how they should be raised, no public schools for instance. They weren't good enough. Andy wanted to be a Boy Scout. All the little boys in the neighborhood had joined a troop, but Bill thought it didn't contain enough boys from families like ours."

"What do you mean, like yours? Mixed?"

"No. How can I put it." She searched for just the right words. "Middle class on the way to upper class. Anyway, we moved shortly after that, so it didn't become a major problem."

"Is that all?" Marva wanted to know.

"He has a way of pigeonholing everybody and everything--the right people, the right schools--our entire lives have to be just right. There have been times when I didn't know what he was looking for.

I'm never sure how far I can go with him in pushing my views." She hunched her shoulders.

"Why?" Karen asked.

"I ask myself, does he want me to be me or does he want me to act like a black wife. I hope you understand what I'm trying to say?"

"No question," Marva said. "Should you be Sapphire or Ms. Ann?"

The three of them laughed again. Then Heleena noticed the puzzled look on Fay's face. "Hey, you don't understand this do you?"

Fay shook her head.

Marva with mock seriousness asked, "Girl where have you been you don't know these famous people?" Not waiting for Fay to respond, she continued. "Well, you are Ms. Ann," she said, pointing her finger at Fay. "And we are Sapphire, in all her glory."

"To be honest, Heleena, you're the first black woman he didn't mind being my friend."

"Her husband protects her from the Sapphire's of this world," Heleena said, still teasing.

"Good thing," Marva said. "Why does he let you continue your friendship with Heleena?"

"Because, Heleena is someone to know."

"Well, excuse me."

"Oh yes. He made sure we got to know her. He viewed Heleena as someone who would not give me silly ideas."

"Just like throwing the rabbit into the briar patch. She's never been the same."

"That is true. Now I feel more comfortable when I express my own opinions to him. I never had much impact on the boys' development. Mark didn't have a difficult time. He flourished despite his father's many opinions about every minute detail of their lives. But, Andy found it hard to always understand what his father wanted from him."

"What do you mean?" Karen asked.

"Well, this race thing. I always thought of my children as black. Bill, on the other hand, believed they were as much white as black, so he pushed them in that direction. But, Andy always gravitated toward black people. I hope I'm not offending anyone."

"No, be specific." Marva said.

"He said they needed to know how to live in a world that is not all black. So that ended my attempts at getting them more in touch with their blackness, as you people say."

"I agree with him on that one," Karen said. "Everything is black this, black that--the whole world isn't black. I encouraged my children to have friendships with more whites. So I sent them to private schools where white people on our level sent their children."

"Were they accepted by the other children?"

"Judy didn't like the school so we moved her."

Heleena and Marva exchanged a knowing look.

* * *

As she pulled the car to a stop at the side door, Heleena saw a huddled figure sitting on the bottom step. She approached the girl. "Honey, why didn't you tell me you were coming?"

Judy stood and put her arms around Heleena, giving her an affectionate hug. "I wanted to see you."

Something in her voice made Heleena look closer. She was just as pretty as ever, but with a haunted look, like a scared animal sensing danger, who didn't know where to run. Her eyes were bright and her hair had begun to unravel from the single plait so carelessly woven. She was wearing one of those granny dresses so popular in the early seventies. The silky tan fabric covered with colorful blue daises clung enticingly to her figure. Her strong young breasts jutted out like cups.

"Come in and we can talk." Heleena sat on a sofa and put a pillow on the floor at her feet. "Sit here."

When Judy was comfortable she began to unplait the plump braid, combing through the thick strands with her fingers.

"Why do you hide such beautiful hair?"

"You and Peter are the only ones who think so."

"It's true. Any girl would love to have a head full of gorgeous hair like yours."

"Not mommie, she's always telling me to brush it down or do something so that it isn't flying all over me."

"She doesn't mean to lessen its beauty, but you came along with so much more hair than she was accustomed to. Remember now, your mom and your aunts keep their hair short and that makes for easier care."

Judy hunched her shoulders.

"Aunt Heleena, tell me about mommie and my dad before I came."

"They were like all couples preparing for the arrival of their second child."

"No, I mean before they had Junior -- when they were young."

Heleena had not expected this, so she said nothing, wondering why had this child, who was like her own, come asking such questions. When she did not respond, Judy slipped off the pillow and turned around to face Heleena, crossing her legs.

Her eyes implored Heleena to speak. "How did daddy win mommie?"

"She wanted your father with a purple passion and let him know how she felt."

"How?"

"When a woman wants a man to notice her she doesn't stand on ceremony or principle, she shows him and tells him." Heleena leaned back and tucked her folded legs under her hips.

"Your dad was a good catch. Karen scoped him out and zeroed in on him like a missile. She made him feel good. He was flattered by her attention, after all she was a very attractive young girl. She was special to him."

"She's still pretty."

"Yes. She is."

"So she really cared about him."

"Yes?"

"Love? Did she love him?"

"Of course she did. Why are you asking me these questions honey? Wouldn't it be better to talk to them about how they met?"

"I don't think they even remember. Sometimes I wonder if they understand."

"Understand what?"

"You know, that deep feeling you get when you're with the person you love."

"You've found that certain person?"

"Yes."

"Peter?"

"The only time I feel good, Aunt Heleena is when I'm with him."

"One thing about caring so much for someone is it's so easy for that person to break your heart."

She lowered her head, shielding her eyes, then just as quickly, threw her head back and the majestic mane exploded around her lovely face. For one second Heleena saw a glimmer of defiance sparkle in her young eyes. During that brief time their eyes held.

"He's everything to me. I won't give him up."

Step carefully, she told herself, her parents have not been able to pry her away from him.

"What is it about Peter you like most?"

"He treats me special, just as you said my dad treated mommie. He listens to me, smiles when he sees me and he talks to me, really talks. When I'm with him, nothing else matters. I can't imagine my life anymore without him."

I should have noticed immediately, the knowing look and new assurance, that self- satisfied confident manner a female assumes when she has left childhood behind.

She's slept with him.

Heleena stood and gently pulled Judy to her feet, wrapping her tightly in her arms.

"Sweetheart, I love you so much."

She pulled back and let her eyes slowly pass from the top of Judy's head to the neat ballerina slippers that covered her narrow feet. There was nothing childlike about her enchantingly rounded body. She cradled the pretty face between her hands and read in those clear eyes solid resolve.

"Aunt Heleena, what was that for?"

"For reminding me how swiftly love can bloom for the young when everything is right."

She gently pinched her cheeks. Blood flowed immediately to the surface, suffusing those dusky cheeks with subdued warm color.

"He's wonderful."

Heleena returned to the sofa. "Tell me more about your Peter?"

"Well, I'm going to Florida to meet his family. I'm so excited."

To her young mind this was a symbol of promise, permanency. Only if he is serious about a woman, will a man have her become involved with his family. There was little doubt Peter knew how to boost her self esteem.

"When?"

"Soon. He hasn't decided the exact date, yet."

"How does Karen feel about this trip?"

The haunted look was back and she vibrated with tension. It was not a fair question for she knew the answer.

"She doesn't like Peter and will not let him in her house," her voice trembled. "Aunt Heleena, you're mommie's best friend, she will listen to you. Will you give him a chance? I wish she'd get to know him the way I do."

That's highly unlikely. The little girl Judy, still wanted her mother's approval, but the woman had already decided her course of action.

She went over to the refrigerator and began to take out something for a snack. When she turned, Judy was staring at her expectantly, twisting the two West Indian bracelets on her arm.

"Sweetheart, I'll do what I can. Your mother is very determined and she really only wants the best for you."

When she finished eating both sandwiches, she looked up at Heleena, waiting for her to say the right words.

"You want me to help persuade your parents to see Peter as you see him, but--"

"Just mommie."

True. "But I don't know Peter. I've only seen him once. The most I can do is ask her to give you some breathing room with him."

Even as she said the words, Heleena knew Karen would not give an inch.

Judy was still toying with the bracelets, waiting for an answer. The heavy gold bangles were two of the six Heleena brought back from the Islands. She'd bought two for each of the teenage girls, her own daughter, Judy and Selena. They were once a close trio, but now each went her separate way.

I have to give her hope. "Let me think about a way to approach your mother that will get her to listen."

"You promise?"

"I promise."

JUNE-JULY- AUGUST

Chapter 4

It took Heleena all of two seconds to say yes. She accepted his invitation so fast she forgot to find out why Marva was back in Alabama. This was not the first time Al had invited her to a social function. Usually, however, the three of them went together. She looked through her closet discarding several outfits, before finally selecting bronze silk pants topped by a leopard print shell.

Her friendship with Al deepened after Greg left. Sharing her feelings with him following the separation and divorce, he shocked her when he told her the divorce hadn't been a surprise to him. "Greg was not the man for you. You were merely a trophy for him."

"I can't believe he married me and didn't love me."

"The point is you were someone who fit perfectly his idea of what a wife should be. Sweetheart, you are a prize."

In their many conversations he'd been warm and understanding, explaining some of the intricacies of a man's personality that caused him to lose self confidence as he approached mid-life. He admitted suffering some doubt about his own life, including his marriage. She was too miserable at the time to comprehend the significance of his admission. According to Marva there were some infidelities. She never gave any details, however. Whether he was faithful to his marriage vows was not a concern for her. He was definitely the kind of man likely to draw women. Even now, if she had questions about a certain guy, she never hesitated to call him and discuss them.

When she opened the door he saw the question in her eyes, "Marva left for Alabama yesterday, it's just you and me. You're not afraid of me are you?"

"Scared to death," she responded playfully. "I thought she was leaving next week."

"She changed her mind."

"That's strange. Why didn't she call me? Is there something wrong with her mom?"

"No."

"Well, what?"

"My company isn't good enough for you, now?"

"You know better," she said, reaching out to gently touch his arm. "What woman wouldn't enjoy being with you. I always said Marva lucked out in a big way," she emphasized her statement by playfully pushing her index finger into his middle.

"No more questions, Okay?" He tapped her lips with a long forefinger, putting an end to the subject.

I wonder if they had another argument about Selena.

His eyes followed her as she moved to close and lock the side patio door.

She turned, catching his look and smiled in return. "Do I need to take anything?"

"Only the determination to enjoy yourself. But, there is something I insist you do."

"What's that?"

"Relax."

"Deal."

His devastating smile caused her a moment of anxiety.

* * *

The used Targa was the first toy he bought when the money started rolling in, eleven thousand dollars, an astronomical sum for a car at that time. Chevies did not cost more than eighty-five hundred dollars. He lavished great love and attention on the car, even to the point of learning to tune it himself.

He had it restored by a dealer in upstate New York who specialized in the restoration of German cars. Ninety percent of the work was done by hand. Everything was original, all the parts, even the paint. She compared car and owner, sleek and powerful.

Once they were out on the highway heading south, she did relax. The small car held its own among the giant behemoths with eighteen wheels. Al expertly accelerated and slowed with ease as traffic demanded.

"What are you thinking?"

"The changes I've seen since I came up here. Seldom do I get a chance to just sit back and enjoy the passing scenery. Remember back in the early seventies when people moved out to Prince George's County how excited we were? Those split level houses were so different from anything in our experience. The idea of a house with more than one level, dishwashers and decks."

He smiled without comment.

"Remember Jerry Jones and Linda? When they moved out to Maryland we thought that was the end of the world. There was almost nothing between the Beltway and the turn-off to 301. Whatever happened to them?"

"After the divorce she and the children went back to South Carolina and Jerry moved to Atlanta. He now lives in St. Thomas. I hear from him every year at Christmas."

"They were a fun couple, happy and so in love."

"Back then, we all were."

She looked at him. "This is the first time I've heard you sound so cynical."

"Heleena, happiness is just a label, a name for comfortable feelings. In the scheme of things its meaningless."

"What do you mean? What scheme of things?"

"In the sense that we all seek comfort, wanting to feel good, safe, secure. Everything we do is to that end. Whether its right is often irrelevant; we tend to push on, trying to stay within that comfort zone."

Is he changing too, like the rest of us?

Across the small space he touched her arm, "Are you happy?"

Am I? Certainly I have all the accoutrements for modern-day happiness. All but one. At this time in my life when I feel I really need a man to share the everyday joys and nuisances, there is no one.

"Are you?"

He did not try to dress it up or explain. "No."

He surprised her with his blunt answer, "Tell it to somebody else Al."

"You haven't answered my question."

"In most areas of my life, I am."

His only response was another gentle touch. They were silent for a time, lost in private thoughts. Dr. Alvin R. Harris, husband, father, rich, movie-star handsome and unhappy? Marva never let on. I'll be damn.

"I can hear you thinking."

She smiled. "Well then, you can hear me wondering what in your world could possibly make you unhappy."

"It's not that I'm unhappy, but not happy in the way I naturally assumed I would be at 53, there's a difference. I'm satisfied most of the time with things as they are simply because of the absence of aggravation. My life is predictable."

She stared at him for a long time, oblivious to the cars and trucks roaring past. She was sure he shared something of himself he hadn't with anyone else.

"Did all your dreams come true?"

"Some have, some haven't. Pursuit of the dream is the real nut of the game. I never really concern myself with whether I'm at a certain point and can say, my dreams have come true."

"That sounds like something I should remember, but I don't quite understand what you mean."

"It's simple. You know what you want, so you go for it, enjoying yourself all the time."

Traffic was heavier now as they neared the Kings Dominion exit, so their progress slowed. Al touched one of the console buttons and the cassette came to life with one of her favorite old ballads. "Boy you had to dig way down to get that one."

"I made this tape for you, including some of the really old stuff."

It was no secret, everyone knew she liked oldies and had an excellent collection of them, some originals. That he had taken the time to make a tape for her was just one more reason to be thankful for his friendship. "This is great, thanks."

As they approached Richmond all of Al's concentration was on maneuvering through the congestion. With very little use of brakes and the car's five gears, he managed to keep moving. They were able to resume their speed after exiting onto 295.

When they arrived it appeared most of the guests were already there. The long drive and car park area contained about twenty cars. Al pulled off onto the grass away from the other vehicles.

They followed the stone steps to the back of the house. Heleena's uneasiness returned, briefly upsetting her calm about this trip. When I enter this house with Al, what will these people think? Has he brought other women to social functions down here? She was thinking so furiously she missed a step and stumbled, falling back against him. Regaining her composure, she put the disturbing thoughts from her mind.

The party was in full swing. The minute they stepped inside the long room several men rushed up to Al, one slapping him on the back, welcoming him into the group.

"Hey, this must be the counselor." He extended his hand to her. "Welcome."

So he'd told them he was bringing his attorney. "Thank you." She assumed he was the owner of this house.

As was her way, she surveyed the crowd. They made a magnificent mosaic, beautiful people, richly dressed and obviously enjoying themselves to the hilt. There was a familiar face across the room. She moved away from Al, slowly making her way through the group, stopping to say hello and introducing herself.

Before she reached her destination, someone grabbed her arm, "Heleena, I thought that was you." She stared, not recognizing him. "It's Jimmy, Jimmy Pace, from law school."

"Oh my God, Jimmy I didn't recognize you. How are you?" She hugged him.

"I'm hanging in here but, I can sure see you're doing a whole lot better than that."

"Do you live in this area?"

"No. I just came for the presentation, same reason you're here."

What the hell is he talking about, what presentation? Just as she was about to ask him, Al came up beside her and the glad-handing resumed. Heleena began to relax, now that she'd found someone she knew among the guests. While smiling and making small talk, her mind moved to another level, recalling images of him when they were in school. He was a year ahead of her. He'd been glib, always posturing, talking too loud. Here he is, years later, unchanged.

With his arm around her waist, Al gently steered her around Jimmy's know-it-all talk, sensing her desire to leave the little group forming around Jimmy. She flashed him a smile of thanks.

When finally they were alone for a few minutes, standing in the corner of the patio, Heleena could wait no longer to find out the real reason for this trip. The longer she held off asking the angrier she became. "Jimmy said something about a presentation. Are we down here for a sales pitch?"

"Apparently. I was under the impression this was just a social gathering. Like you, I keep hearing talk about a presentation. I have no idea what it is. We'll just have to wait and see."

She felt better. A part of her felt disappointed at the thought Al had invited her for the sole purpose of listening to someone trying to get his hands into her purse.

Guests were constantly arriving. An air of expectation emanated from the group. The smoky smell of food cooking on the grill filtered inside making her hungry. She knew, however, no food would be served until they heard the real reason they'd been invited.

The host began moving through the group, pointing them outside. Uh, huh. Here it comes.

Wrought iron tables and chairs were placed in a semi-circle around the pool. They found two seats together at the far end.

After another effusive welcome, the host introduced the guest presenter, an outdated bozo, with shoulder length oily hair. In the time honored tradition of a master pitchman, he began to prance back and forth.

Under the table she squeezed Al's knee and looked at him with a can-you-believe-this grin on her face. He winked in understanding. Her surprise at seeing this character caused her to miss his name so she was content to think of him as Bozo.

He introduced a plan to get his hands on their money. The minute he described the strategy of paying into a fund, Heleena knew it was a pyramid scheme, a sham. She almost laughed aloud at the thought of being here, listening to this outrageous bullshit.

To make money using Bozo's plan a person had to start at the back of the airplane with the contribution of Five Thousand Dollars. Another Three Thousand moved you to the middle section. An additional Two Thousand moved you to first class. Voila! A measly One Thousand more moved you to the pilot's seat. Once there the pilot received not only his Eleven Thousand, but an additional sum for each person he brought in who moved to the pilot's chair. For those temporarily short of funds Bozo was prepared to arrange a loan. He had the notes for them to sign right there on the table and he slapped his hand down on a stack of papers for emphasis. An excited ripple passed through the crowd.

These are intelligent, educated people and they are staring, enthralled, at a con artist, who promises, a big payback if they persuade their friends to sign up by plunking down the initial Five Thousand. Bozo was smarter than she thought. He knew this type, two, in some cases, three mortgages on their homes, credit cards up to the max and perpetually late car payments. He knew easy pickings.

The host assisted Bozo in passing around the notes. Lo and behold every one began filling them out except a couple at the next table.

"Feel like walking down to the river?"

"I never thought you'd ask."

Without ceremony, they left the group and walked toward the riverbank. When they were out of earshot of the others, she whispered, "Was that for real?"

"You better believe it. I'd never believe Donnie would be involved in something like this, after all he's been through."

They stood together watching the slow-moving river. She was standing close to him in an intimate way she secretly enjoyed. They were out of sight of the group, surrounded by tall ancient trees. It was a spot made for the quiet, intimate sharing of secrets.

The breeze was ever so slight. Busy insects drifted by doing their eternal work, flower to flower. Sunlight playfully crept around the leaves, shinning just enough that she felt comfortable hiding behind her sunglasses. Even the seductive smell of honeysuckles pulled at her senses.

No one followed them and she doubted if anyone even missed them. She stepped out of her sandals and waded into the cool water. There were tiny fishes darting around her naked toes. They tickled and she stirred the water shushing them away, only to have them return, unafraid. Heleena felt young again, soft and vulnerable as a spring day slipping gently into evening shadows.

Her back to him, Al watched her closely, but what he saw and the thoughts passing through his mind were those of a younger man whose eyes took pleasure looking on a beautiful woman. Without shame his body reacted. He was no stranger to women and Heleena was no ordinary woman. If he did not know better, he would never believe she was the mother of three grown children. His breath caught as she turned and smiled.

When he stepped up behind her placing his hands on each side of her waist, she swayed, thrilling to his touch, then moved away. They walked slowly along the edge of the water.

The shadows deepened in places where trees shut out the sun. An eerie spell tightened its web around them. Heleena was both, afraid and excited. Unerringly, Al sensed her fear, he knew her well. Adroitly he guided them back the way they'd come. "We don't want to miss any of this, now do we?"

They returned to the group to find Bozo had collected all his notes and was now circulating among the guests continually assuring them of impossible returns on their borrowed money.

They looked like characters, with painted on grins, showing too many teeth and laughing too loudly. She heard snippets of conversation extolling the benefits of private school over public school, the cost of cars, and other elitist notions common to middle class blacks. One of the people who sat next to her during the presentation gave himself a verbal pat on the back for sending his child to a college with extortious costs. And he'd signed a note to give monkey-man thousands of dollars.

Back in the house, Heleena maneuvered her way through several adjoining rooms, admiring the decor. Much time and money went into these furnishings.

She noticed the gaudy tennis bracelets, expensive leather handbags and fine gold necklaces worn by most of the women. They were dressed in today's cultural uniform for the forties and fifties set, yet these people had to borrow money to give a con man.

She settled next to Al on the sofa. Only now he was chatting with a young woman perched on the low arm of the sofa. She introduced herself.

The other woman seemed surprised, however she reached across Al and accepted Heleena's outstretched hand. "I'm Chia from Atlanta."

Using all the aplomb she could muster with this woman who was obviously panting after Al; she asked, "Did you come all this way just to get in on the action?"

"Actually I was up here visiting a friend and we heard about the party from some other people. We tagged along with them,"

"Well, what do you think?"

"The way he explained it, a person could really make some money."

"Did you buy into the plan?"

"My friend and I are going fifty-fifty. She signed the paper. My credit isn't too good right now, but I know I could make money off this."

Heleena could not help herself, "How?"

"All we need to do is find ten more people."

"And each one of them has to bring in ten people, you know."

Chia looked astonished that Heleena could doubt the possibility. "I can name ten of my relatives who would be interested, right now, especially since they can borrow the money."

"Good luck," Heleena said, more as a dismissal than really wishing her well.

Hours later as they said their good-byes, a full moon was high in the sky. The gleaming Porsche came easily to life with the engine purring in perfect time.

As they drove north, Heleena's pleasure was expansive. A smile lit her face in the dark. The fact that she'd convinced herself before she left that the trip was okay; she felt relaxed and unintimidated.

"Thanks for the invite. I had a great time."

"Donnie's a good guy. He likes to accommodate people. That's his way, I am sure someone asked him to have that presentation and he naturally said yes. He was a yes-man to everything his ex-wife wanted and it sent him spiraling into bankruptcy."

"Who was the woman acting so officious, his new wife?"

"No, just a friend. He hasn't remarried."

She continued probing about people at the cook-out. "There was a strange mix at the party. I noticed a group of young women, together. Very young," she emphasized.

"The four who set at the front of the pool?"

"Yes. They didn't seem to fit with that group. Short tight dresses, all that hair and hoop earrings. What were they doing there with a group of middle age people?"

"Out for a good time. It makes the mix interesting anyway."

"I suppose so."

"My only concern is you, that you enjoyed yourself."

"Do you think Marva would have enjoyed it?"

"No. It wasn't her kind of group."

"Most of those people are professionals. Why is it they're sitting in a group listening to some scam artist? That's crazy."

"They're just trying to get ahead."

"You can't get ahead with a scam. Then they had to borrow the money to get into the game."

"Why are you so riled up about this?"

"Because it is so stupid."

"Being stupid isn't a crime."

"Al, these people are educated. How can they fall for a silly little man jumping around with long greasy curls?"

"Human nature."

"It is still a stupid idea."

"Maybe, maybe not. It's not our problem."

"You're right. I don't know why their stupidity should make me so mad. Anyway, I enjoyed hanging out with you, even among those jerks."

She leaned her head back and rubbed her forehead.

"Is anything wrong? You've been having headaches lately."

"It's creeping stress."

"Why?"

"I'm restless and getting more so every day. Right now I'm not exactly satisfied with the direction my life is taking. Or I should say the lack of direction."

"You can make any changes you want."

"It isn't that easy. One of the concerns I have is my career. I'm tired of the firm life. It's been so good to me I get a guilty feeling every time I think about walking away. But, it no longer satisfies me. I go through the business on automatic pilot. My enthusiasm is gone and so is the excitement."

"Sweetheart you can do whatever you want. Maybe there's something else you can do within the firm's wide range of activities."

If that were all, I'd make the appropriate changes. But it's not just the professional side of my life." She was quiet for a moment. "I want more, more personal satisfaction."

When he didn't respond, she looked at him and asked. "Well, what do you think? Do I sound silly?"

"No. You have every right to question where your life is going. Just don't pile guilt on yourself. Make the changes you need to make. One thing you can be sure of; you always have my support."

"And that is the only thing I'm sure of right now."

"Don't ever forget it."

"Thanks."

"This restlessness you feel, I sense there's more to it than what you've said." He sensed she was holding back, which was unusual. "Come on, tell me."

"I've said this to you before, what I really want, is companionship, a man of my own, someone like -- well, just someone for myself."

"What led to this?"

She thought she heard disbelief or disapproval in his voice. "Don't make fun of me. I'm serious."

"I know you are. But what brought it on? Why now?"

"It's time. And I'm ready."

"There are many slick guys out here, looking for someone like you. You have more to lose than you know."

"My God, you are serious."

"Of course I am. You sure you're not just lonely living in that big house all by yourself?"

"There are times when I do miss the kids, but not to the point of having them move back home. It's like I don't have a life. Something's missing."

"A man?"

"Exactly." Her hands became animated trying to explain the urgency she felt. "I want more to my life Al, more living, more excitement, something different."

The calm of his voice betrayed his concern for her. "And you should have anything you want. Just be careful."

"Oh, I won't run out and take up with the first man who looks interesting. I did that once and look how that ended."

"Greg wasn't a bad husband."

"No, he wasn't, but the marriage was wrong--you've said as much yourself. When he asked me to marry him, I was in love--I guess--so I said yes. After all, my closest friends were married, you and Marva, Scooter and Karen. I didn't spend any time considering whether I really wanted marriage at the time. It turned out to be a union where we respected each other, were good parents, had the best of material goods."

"But?"

"You know the meaning of the but. All the good in our marriage could not offset the mismatch. We were wrong for each other."

"Your marriage may not have been as atypical as you think. There were many marriages begun in those days that never should have happened."

"Please," she laughed.

"Believe me, I know."

Chapter 5

As she was about to put her overnight bag in the car the phone rang.

"What's taking you so long?" Karen sounded agitated. "I thought you were coming early so we could talk."

That is precisely why I did not come early. "I was just leaving. My things are in the car. I'll see you in about twenty minutes. We'll have plenty of time." She hung up before Karen could say anything further.

She ought to leave Judy alone and let her live her own life. Hopefully, by the time I get there the other guests will have arrived and I won't have to rehash last week's conversation. She dallied in the kitchen for another fifteen minutes. When she finely arrived Karen followed her right up to the room she used whenever she stayed overnight.

Everyone was gathered in the immense rec-room on the ground floor. Already the women were sitting together on one side of the room and the men on the other.

Heleena knew everyone, except a man and woman on the other side of the room: a tall good looking guy whose eyes quickly locked on hers and a woman sitting on the floor next to the fireplace. She looked away, uncomfortable with his proprietary stare.

Walking directly to Scooter, she kissed him on the cheek, "Hi."

"You know everybody, don't you?"

"Not quite." Her eyes went immediately to the man she'd first noticed.

Scooter followed her stare. "Come over here and let me introduce you to Mario."

"Mario, this is Heleena."

"Very pleased to meet you Mario. How are you?" She liked the sound of his name.

"Better now." He extended his hand, a questioning look on his handsome face.

"Oh, Heleena, Heleena Walton," Scooter finished the introduction.

"And how are you, Heleena?" He asked as he steered her to the seat next to his.

"I'm fine, just fine."

"No question about that."

She laughed and moved to sit beside him. Hmm, this guy is quick on the trigger. She was flattered anyway. Instead of sitting on the wide hassock, she slid to the floor.

"Mario is an interesting name. Italian?"

"By way of Puerto Rico."

"Really?"

"Italian slave owners. My people landed first in the area now known as Puerto Rico. When they were brought to this country someone with an Italian connection bought them. Each succeeding generation kept some part of the ancestral name."

"What is your last name?"

"Just an ordinary Newton."

"Well, Mr. Mario Newton, It looks like you have a very interesting history to pass on to your children."

"Dr. Mario Newton."

"I stand corrected, Dr. Mario."

Uh oh, we're entering jerkdom.

"Thanks. I paid in blood for that title."

"I know you did."

In three seconds he let her know the essentials. Never at a loss for polite conversation, she continued, "Where do you practice?"

"Los Angeles." .

"What brings you East?"

"A conference."

"Well Mario, I hope your conference goes well, and that you enjoy yourself."

She turned to chat with the couple on her right. "It's nice seeing you again."

"You too. We see your car from time to time, when you're here."

"This house is like a second home for me. I'm always in and out."

As she stood and walked away she felt Mario's eyes following her. She joined a small knot of women sitting near the fireplace. They were talking about their young adult children who were reluctant to leave home.

"I go to the store three or four times a week," someone said.

Scooter's partner's wife, Ruth, had a cure for these young people. "My position is this, at twenty-one if they're in school they can stay. If they're out of school they have to leave."

"That seems cruel," Anna Jean interjected.

In unison they looked at her, no one quite knowing what to say. Anna Jean was a second wife, whose only child had always lived with his natural father and the children of her current husband were not welcomed for any prolonged stays with her and their father.

Ruth sighed and continued, "When you have done time with the boy scouts, girl scouts, little league baseball, soccer, football, dance and piano lessons, then Anna Jean you can set limits and stick to your guns."

Anna Jean did not know when to leave well enough alone. "I didn't mean you shouldn't put limits on kids, it's just that to throw them out in the world before they are ready seems pretty cruel to me."

"Like I said, when you," Ruth placed exaggerated emphasis on you, "raise a child, then you can give an opinion."

The woman Heleena had never seen now chimed in. "What do you do when the kids come back, stay a while, leave, then repeat the process again?"

"Is that how your children avoid breaking the cord?" Heleena asked her.

"No. I don't have any children. My boyfriend's children come and go like that."

Ruth opened her mouth, but swallowed her retort, almost choking.

"He doesn't mind, but it plays havoc with his social life. That's the reason I came with him on this trip. We needed to have some time together. I think his ex-wife encourages them just for spite."

Ruth could not contain herself any longer, "I wonder why?"

"Who is your boyfriend?" Heleena asked, looking around the room.

"Mario."

So you are with Mario. Well, well, well. "Do you travel with him often?"

"Two or three times a year."

Must be nice. "Getting away together like that has to be fun and relaxing."

"It is. But more than fun it gives us time to cement our relationship. Women are forever chasing him."

"Some of them think single guys are up for grabs, even if they're in a steady relationship."

"Sometimes, even if they are in a marriage."

The music was getting louder and two couples were now dancing. For a few minutes the group gave full attention to the dancers.

"I like that song," someone said.

"The version by Areatha is better."

Karen rose and stood between the group clustered around the fireplace and the group of mostly guys seated on the sofas and chairs in the middle of the room. "Come on everybody. Let's go. It's time to dance." She pulled Scooter from his seat and they began to move to the beat of the music.

"You two can still do it," someone hollered.

"Come on you people," Karen beckoned them.

"Okay, but I need a partner," Heleena said through the funnel of her hands.

"And you have one," Mario said, gently pulling her from the floor.

He moves well, good rhythm.

The next record by the Four Tops brought everybody to their feet -- "Sugar Pie, Honey Bunch."

Mario put his hands on each side of her waist and drew her closer so that they moved together, only inches apart.

He is trying to flirt with me right in front of his girlfriend. Her thoughts did not show on her face. She was smiling and having fun. He looked good, seemed to enjoy her company and she certainly enjoyed his.

"Whoa," he said as she attempted to walk away at the end of the song. "Let's do it again."

"Okay."

"You're a good dancer, really good."

"Thanks. We make a good team on the dance floor."

As they moved together Al touched Mario on the shoulder and they switched partners. Mario caught the beat with Marva.

He moved in perfect time with the music. Had he not gone into medicine, Al could surely have made a career for himself in music. His music was still an essential part of his life, a sure way for him to unwind.

"Are you drifting away from me? I see that deep-in-thought-look on your face."

"No," she laughed. "I was just thinking what great musical timing you have, the way you move with the music."

He raised his eyebrows. "Honest?"

"You know you do."

He spun her around, catching her just as the song ended. As she headed for the bar to get something cool to drink, Mario pulled her back to the dance area. "One more time."

Thankfully, the record had a slower beat.

"I notice you all have a lot of fun together."

"Oh yes, it doesn't take a special occasion for us to do things like this. We enjoy each other."

"It's unusual when people stay close for such a long time."

"What worked for us is we've stayed in the same area, so we're not physically separated by more than a few miles."

"Tell me Heleena, are you married, divorced or...?"

"He'd caught her off guard and she missed a step. "Excuse me."

"No problem."

"I'm divorced. Why do you ask?" She wasn't accustomed to people asking about her marital status because most of the people who knew her, knew she and Greg were no longer married.

"Is there a man in your life, you know, a significant other?"

She groaned inwardly at the reference to significant other. It was a stupid term. "No. Why?"

"A woman like you? That seems unlikely."

Oh boy, I have to follow this just to be polite. "What is a woman like me?"

"Don't get coy on me now. You know exactly what I mean."

"No I don't. Tell me."

"First of all, you are an attractive woman, desirable. A man would naturally notice you, right off the bat."

"There are hundreds of women like me around, thousands."

"Let me finish."

"Go ahead."

"You're smart."

"How do you know that? You just met me. You don't know anything about me."

"You're a lawyer."

"Ha."

He shrugged his shoulders. Well, my experience is that lawyers are clever. And there is something about you that just naturally attracts a man."

"I'm humbled."

"See, a response like that intrigues me. Most women would simply accept a compliment with a thank you. But, your response is totally different. It's that quality about you that gives the impression you don't take yourself seriously."

"I don't."

"You're a rare breed then."

The music had stopped, but they were standing in the middle of the floor, still moving slightly to the beat of a song no longer playing.

There is more depth to him than first appears.

"Hey you two," someone yelled, "you can let go now, that dance has ended."

Not to be undone, Mario called back, "Just getting a little free legal advice."

"Scooter, who was not known for his humor, teased, "If you stand there much longer, you'll have to pay $400.00 for the first hour."

Mario raised both hands in surrender. "The clock just stopped."

Heleena moved to the table and gathered a small plate of cut raw vegetables. "Okay you guys, watch your manners."

She then squeezed on the sofa between Carolyn and Marva. Leaning across Marva, she whispered for Al's ears only. "What's the story with Mario?"

"Which story?"

"You know. What's the deal with him? At first he comes on like a Romeo, but then he seems like a really nice guy. Is he that nice person or the Romeo?"

"You're interested?"

"Kind of."

"He's not for you."

"That is not what she asked you," Marva interjected. This was not the first time she'd heard them go through this routine.

"My answer is still the same. He is not the type of man you need."

"Heleena decided to take a different tact. "He is single, isn't he?"

"Oh, yes."

"How serious is he with what's-her-name from Los Angeles?"

"Listen Heleena, Mario is an all right kind of guy, but he is definitely a ladies man. You can strike him immediately."

"When will you learn not to ask him to stamp his approval on someone who sparks your interest?" Marva asked her.

"Well, he knows most of these people -- details about them."

Marva shook her head in a gesture of futility.

"Look, he's charming, but as many other women have found, he will not commit. Forget him."

"Okay, I wanted to know the truth."

"So now you know. Let him take his bag of tricks back to LA"

She sat back and began to eat her food.

"You're never going to get another man if you continue to ask for Al's approval."

"You just might be right. He's never given it yet."

"When you find somebody interesting you'd better go after him and tell Al about him later."

Heleena knew Marva was right. But tonight Al appeared annoyed that she found Mario interesting. Mario was now dancing with his girlfriend.

"What's her name?"

"Renea."

"She's a beautiful woman."

"She is."

"How old do you think she is?"

"At or near our age. I heard her say she'd been teaching school for twenty-one years."

"Really? She looks much younger."

"Gee, so do we, I hope."

"I don't know, sometimes I feel older."

"Me too, but that doesn't make us look old. Anyway, I don't want to sit here and talk about getting old."

"That's okay for you to say, but I have to consider it. You have a man, me, I have only a wish. Men want younger women."

"That's probably true, but you don't have to sound desperate."

The look Heleena gave her was a cross between incredulousness, hurt and confusion. "What are you talking about? I'm not desperate."

"You're starting to sound like it." She left the sofa and headed for the stairs.

Heleena moved closer to Al as though she were seeking protection from an unseen enemy. He, in turn, attempted to assure her. "You don't have to worry about getting a man and you definitely don't need to concern yourself with age, okay?"

"I'll take your word. Thanks."

Without another word, he too went to the table and began to fill his plate.

A communal hush fell over the party room as they ate.

Heleena helped Karen carry drinks to the guests. Then they sat together on the bottom step.

"I noticed you and Mario were getting a little cozy on the dance floor."

"Not really. We were just talking; getting to know each other. He's an interesting guy. You could say he has a way with women."

"Hah, that's a laugh. Mario has three girlfriends at any time. He always has and always will. When he was in school, he lived with a woman his last year. Evidently, he'd promised to marry her. Well, after graduation he flew home to Los Angeles to begin his internship, promising to send for her as soon as he found a place. Two months later he married another woman he'd been going with all the time."

"What?"

"It was a common occurrence back then. Graduation day some woman apparently out of the blue would show up and they'd marry immediately. The girlfriend who supported him financially and every other way during school, was left holding the bills, lease and dirty laundry. You ought to remember some of this. There were even a couple of suicides after graduation."

"What ever happened to Mario's girlfriend?"

"Who knows? She had her heart broken and hopefully she recovered. Just consider this, here he is flirting with you while his date is sitting in the same room."

After the big feast everyone set around listening to the music until Marvin Gaye and Tammy Terrell sang the first words of "The Real Thing." Then half the party rose, even the two white couples.

As coffee was served, some of the men loosened their belts a notch or two. The group was older now and no longer felt pressured to dance up a healthy sweat. They were comfortable without having to push the good time issue.

"Can you believe these are the same people who once partied until daybreak? Look at them now, just like contented pussycats," Karen commented.

"I was thinking the same thing. And we still had plenty of energy for whatever else we wanted to do."

"The years have added up and exacted their toll."

"At least now we don't have to worry about the babies when we're out having a good time." The words were out before Heleena realized how Karen would interpret them.

Karen did not let the innocent statement pass. "You may not have to worry about your babies anymore, I'm still worrying about mine."

"I know you're thinking about Judy, but she'll be okay. Just let up on her a bit."

"She's drifting and it seems we can't help her. At least she won't accept our advice."

"They all go through that time of life."

Before Karen responded, Carolyn came up behind them carrying a tray of dirty dishes. Again, Heleena was thankful for the interruption. She knew Karen was ready to launch into another discussion about Judy and her man.

Two hours later, Carolyn, her date, Marva, Al, Scooter, Karen and Heleena sat around the room comparing tonight's party with the parties they had twenty years ago, remembering people who no longer played in their lives.

* * *

Heleena sitting in bed cushioned by pillows at her back, barely heard the light knock. "Come in." She looked up from the magazine in her hands, her glasses resting on the bridge of her nose.

"Karen, let Heleena go to sleep," Scooter yelled down the hall.

"I will," she called back, but came in anyway and sat at the foot of the bed.

Heleena closed the magazine and removed her glasses. Well, here it comes, more complaints about Judy.

"It sure was nice to see Willie and Cora. I haven't seen them in ages."

"They've been keeping a low profile. Things haven't gone well for them lately. Willie's company let him go."

"I thought he was in the upper echelon of management."

"He was, but they cut him just the same. He went from a six-figure salary to zip and Cora's salary is really not able to sustain them. A teacher's salary can go up just so much."

He found a position at another company, but they reorganized after six months and he was out of a job again. Cora said they're living off his severance pay, but it'll run out soon."

"What are they going to do?"

"She doesn't know. Enough about them, I need to discuss my baby."

"What's going on with her now?"

"The latest thing is her planned trip to Florida. I think she's going with her boyfriend."

Heleena didn't let on that she knew about the trip. "So, what's wrong with that? I know you're thinking we never even thought about traveling with a man when we were her age. But, this is a new day."

"It's more than that. He is no good and he is definitely no good for her. Anytime we try to talk to her about him she becomes snappish and angry. Now, Scooter won't bring up the subject anymore. It's only me trying to reason with her. That's why I wish you'd talk to her."

"But what can I say to her that you haven't already said? I've seen this guy only once and he was sitting outside in his car. I spoke and he returned the greeting. That is the extent of my knowledge of him." She leaned forward, lifting both of her hands, palms up, in a gesture of futility.

"Heleena please. You're the only person she might believe."

"Believe what?"

"That Peter is no good for her, that he is a bad influence."

Scooter's knock on the door stopped Karen's further pleas.

He came in wearing a brown and beige striped silk robe and sat opposite Karen at the foot of the bed. "I knew she'd be in here pressuring you about Judy. I keep telling Karen to let her alone. She's got to make decisions for herself."

"I'm not trying to make decisions for her. I wish you all would just listen to me, think about what's happening to her."

"Nothing's happening to her, honey." He reached for her hand and squeezed lovingly.

"What do you call not coming home at night, not even saying where she is going, or who with."

"Oh, we know who with."

"You know what I mean. She's pulling away from us. Now, she's planning to go to Florida and hasn't even told us. I overheard her talking to that snake."

"You mean you were eavesdropping."

"Call it whatever you want, but I heard her."

Scooter rolled his eyes and hunched his shoulders.

"I thought you would learn by now. Your meddling in Junior's, life drove him away from us. Now, you're doing the same thing with Judy."

"Maybe you should ease the pressure on her," Heleena suggested.

"Since you won't listen to me, at least listen to Heleena." He reached across and squeezed her hand again, then walked around to the other side of the bed. "Come on let's go to bed so Heleena can get to sleep." He pulled his wife to her feet and steered her toward the bedroom door.

Heleena turned off the lamp next to her bed, but she lay awake for a long time, staring into the dark. Even Karen's constant nagging doesn't affect Scooter's love for her.

* * *

Pricey Roland Park was only blocks away. York Road with its trendy shops farther out. Same street, but at this point it's called Greenmount, a misnomer, since there is not one blade of green grass in sight.

The couple stood together in the alley behind row houses that had seen better days, amid trash, broken bottles, and cans. She was standing behind him, her arms around his waist. The beautiful girl was full of happiness and it shone on her face as only the love of a young girl can.

The man, on the other hand stood with an air of detachment, a look of disdain on his face. Whether for the girl or his surroundings, one could not tell.

"How much longer will we have to wait?"

He patted her clasped hands as if to humor her. "You said you wanted to spend this time with me. Now don't be impatient."

"I wasn't being impatient. I just want to know when we can go back to the apartment."

"We will go back when we go back," he replied with annoyance.

Judy didn't say anything else. She was satisfied being with him, no matter where they were. Her only happiness was the time she spent with Peter. If he agreed, she would move in with him, but every time she brought it up, he said no.

"The time is not right yet," he told her."We can't make that move before I get another apartment, simply because your parents could not stomach the idea of you living in such quarters." He emphasized quarters as if it were a dirty word.

"It doesn't matter what they think," she said feebly.

"It'll be soon enough."

They heard someone walking along the side of the rowhouse toward the alley where they were standing. She immediately felt Peter's body stiffen. The tension in him was alive. She did not know that tonight he was receiving payment for a delivery of assault weapons.

Peter knew how to stay in the background. Putting illegal guns on the streets of Baltimore proved easier than even he figured. He never personally went into Virginia, but the .9 mm pistols now coming onto the streets were tied directly to his actions. The guns brought anywhere between $200.00 -- $1,500.00 each.

Judy never questioned him about his business. She would never even think to wonder why they were standing in this filthy dark alley. Searching for love and acceptance all her life, Peter took her just as he found her. There was no talk of changing hairstyles or not wearing red lipstick because it made her lips look too big. He touched those lips, kissed them and made her heart sing.

As the footsteps came closer, Peter made two short whistle sounds. The same sounds were immediately returned.

Unlocking her hands from his waist, Peter whispered, "Wait here." He was sure of her obedience. She did not disappoint him.

He went to the corner of the building. Without saying a word, he accepted a compact package.

"It's all there," the other man said quietly, his West Indian accent noticeable.

"I don't doubt it, *mon*."

As with most of his enterprises, he relied mainly on his countrymen. He did not have to count the money, if there was a discrepancy retribution would be quick and lethal. In the world of drugs and guns there was only one way to settle disputes.

He saw the two silhouettes at the end of the driveway to the alley. Following the direction of his companion's eyes, he received assurance. "Joe and Mackey," the other man said. "They okay, from Miami." He nodded his head in Judy's direction, a question in his eyes.

"Judy," Peter said.

"See you next week then."

"Take care *mon*."

With the packet under his arm, Peter returned to her. As always her welcoming smile for him was true, even after so short a separation. Taking her hand they quickly returned to the beat-up looking old Chevy Nova. No sleek Jeep Cherokee or Pathfinder for him. Just an old clunker that would go unnoticed by police.

* * *

This was one of those rare occasions when Karen actually talked with Scooter instead of talking at him. So he knew she was troubled.

"Why are you worried about her going to Florida? My God, she's twenty-four, she's gone away before by herself."

"That's just it, she isn't going alone."

"Even so, what can we do? Judy is a grown woman. We can't prohibit her movements; you know that."

"But, we've got to do something. I feel her withdrawing further and further from us. I'm really worried Scooter, and scared."

"You talked to Heleena, what does she think?"

"She feels the same as you. Every time I ask her to talk to Judy I can see the reluctance on her face."

"That should tell you something."

"This is my baby we're talking about and where her welfare is concerned, I will not be dissuaded from wanting to help her."

"Please honey, can't you see what it's doing to her. We never see her anymore and when she is at home she stays locked in her room."

"Doesn't that raise your concern?"

"Look, its plain she is going through some type of emotional upheaval. I don't know what's causing it and neither do you. She's still growing up and maturing. She has to work out her problems herself, unless she comes to us for help. Whatever this man means to her, there is absolutely nothing we can do."

"She'll never talk to us."

"Do you ever wonder why that is so?"

"Of course. Why do you think I'm so worried now? I just wish all of you would believe me."

He walked over to her, pulled her from the bed and held her face between his hands. "Whatever you do, please promise me you won't drive her away, like Junior."

"It wasn't my desire to drive him away."

Scooter dropped his hands in resignation. He'd been down this road before tonight. Karen was hardheaded.

"Promise me you will lighten up?" He asked her again.

Those thin lips she was so proud of now set in a narrow straight line. "I can't make that promise. I wish you wouldn't ask me."

He kept quiet as they readied themselves for bed. She meant good, but whenever she tried to act on what she felt was for the children's good; it always seemed to backfire. He never interfered with her actions when the children were younger. Maybe I should have. He'd always thought it was his position to work and provide for all their needs, but what nagged him now, was whether he had given them enough of himself. He set on the side of the bed.

"What are you thinking?" She was already in bed.

"Just about the children and asking myself if I've been the father I should have been to them." He slipped in beside her, then reached above the bed to turn out the light.

"You sure don't have to worry about that. You did everything for them you could have done. If it weren't for you they couldn't have had the opportunities they had. We denied them nothing."

"That is what worries me."

"Why should it?"

"Maybe I gave them everything but enough of myself."

"You made a good life for us. How else could we live like this?" Even though he could not see her gesture in the darken room, she spread her arms wide, encompassing the house and all it represented.

"I thought that's what I was doing, then I think about my own father, who worked for white people all his life, eeking out a living to provide for us. And he did a good job."

"What does that have to do with our lifestyle?"

"Everything."

"What? Tell me." She rose on her elbow, looking down at him, impatient with his reasoning once again.

"We were close to my father. We respected him and my mother. We would never think of defying them."

"Life is different now. The world is different. Children are different.

"True, but relationships between parents and their children should not be different. You'd think with all we've spent on making life comfortable for them, shielding them from the rough grip of racism; we would not find ourselves at this point wondering why we can't talk to our children. Or why they won't listen to us."

"I do everything I can for them so I know it's not my fault Judy is having problems."

Scooter was laying flat on his back, ankles crossed, with his hands cushioning his head. He looked at the ceiling but was seeing something else. "Remember when we decided to get married and I wanted to tell our parents, and you said, let's wait and tell them afterward."

"I remember."

"I knew my mother and father would be hurt. Not knowing your people I didn't know how they'd feel, but I suspected they wouldn't be happy with the situation."

"They were pleased and immediately welcomed you into the family."

"In their way."

"What do you mean, in their way?"

"You didn't exactly bring home the type of person they expected you to, in a general sense."

"Well right now, you're not making any sense."

"Karen, you know exactly what I mean. You brought home a husband who was as black as tar. And for years, as I got to really know them, I was always surprised they actually accepted me."

"Geez, after all, you were guaranteed to make a good life for me, a lot of money."

"Why should that have made a difference? I loved you, married you and expected to be a good husband to you."

"And you have. I could never complain about you."

"I learned, of course, that was my saving grace. It didn't matter what they thought about me, but I always resented their comments about Junior and Judy."

"You don't still hold that against them do you?"

"Oh, yes I do. I can still hear your aunt, Reba Mae, and your cousin discussing and wondering out loud about what color Judy would be. Eva had the nerve to say that the worse that could happen is she wouldn't be any darker that Junior."

"You need to let that go?"

As if he hadn't heard her, Scooter continued, "Then Reba Mae said, yes, but he is a man; he can get away with being dark. Look at his daddy, he got Karen didn't he? And they laughed like it was some kind of joke."

"Please."

"I think much of Judy's opinion of herself stems from all the little comments and digs they make about color."

"They're not always talking about her."

"No, they may not refer to her specifically every time, but they always manage to bring color into the picture when they're discussing anyone. So and So is too dark for that color; she needs to stay out of the sun; this old black nigger or that old black nigger -- how do you think it makes her feel, when they've already told her she's too dark?"

"She isn't exactly black, she has more of an olive complexion."

"No. She isn't black but she sure isn't light enough for your people."

"I don't think you're being fair."

"Fair has nothing to do with anything. What can Judy think when she hears her own grandmother say, and I quote, 'Nannie never let any black niggers sit in that chair, she claimed the color of their asses would rub off like ink, then you could never get it clean again.' Another family joke. They tell that story over and over again, every time that chair is mentioned."

"Is that why you wouldn't let me bring it here even though everybody knew she wanted me to have it?"

"There have been few times I've denied you anything, since the day I first saw you. But, that chair was something I could not live with."

She had no response, so she lay quietly, also starring at the ceiling.

Both had been silent for a while, when she asked him, "Tell the truth, weren't you excited about my light skin? Think about it? Don't you remember what you told me once?"

When he didn't answer, she continued. "You said it was exciting to you when you lay in bed, holding me and making love, to see your dark skin entangled with my light skin. You said you could get off just by thinking about it."

"And do you remember what you said?"

"No."

"You said, get off all you want, just don't let that black sweat leave any stains on me."

"I was only joking. But you still found my skin color enticing and exciting, didn't you? Admit it."

"I was a young buck, I said and did a lot of foolish things back then."

Karen sat up and clicked the light switch over their heads. She leaned over him. "Was it foolish for you to tell me whatever it was about me that you found desirable?"

"I didn't mean it like that. What you looked like, of course has much to do with my attraction to you. You were beautiful and you still are. It's just that your family emphasizes color above all else in their relations with people. I've never been comfortable around them, but I adjusted. What I can't tolerate are all their comments about Judy's color and what a problem it will be for her."

"She didn't take what they said as gospel."

"There is a slim chance you may be right. I hope you are, however, an impressionable child like Judy internalizes what people think about her, especially her family."

Karen lay back on her pillow, but left the light burning. "You always find fault with my relatives. You seem to forget that I'm part of that same family."

"I haven't forgotten. Since you've been away from them most of your adult life you have escaped their worse tendencies."

"Thanks," she said without much conviction.

"Not all though. Your tendency to put people down has also affected Judy. When was it we first noticed her shyness and tendency to retreat into herself?"

"Just after she turned fourteen. I remember it well." "There was that African boy at her school who she liked. She was very fond of him -- talking to him on the phone endlessly."

"That was her first crush on a boy or at least the first one we knew about."

"He was a nice kid from a nice family. He had only one draw back according to you."

"What?"

"He was too black, like charcoal you said, and his hair was beady."

"Well it was true."

"But did you have to say that to Judy?"

"No harm was done."

"I'm not so sure. But I did notice the abrupt change in her. Maybe she told him what you said, because he stopped calling. I know other boys called but her responses to them lacked her previous enthusiasm. She became quieter and withdrawn."

"It may have been because of some other reason."

"Maybe, but that is the event I will always associate with her change. Judy was always a beautiful child, still is. And I'm not saying so because she's my daughter. Everybody who sees her comments about her looks."

"She'd look better if she just did something with that hair."

"There you go. That's what I'm talking about. You find fault with everything. Some women would kill to have beautiful thick hair like Judy's"

"I'm not saying there is anything wrong with her hair. She just doesn't know or doesn't care how to wear it to the best advantage."

"According to you."

"Anybody would agree that one long braid hanging down her back is not an attractive way for a young girl to wear her hair. First of all, she needs to cut about three inches."

"One thing is for sure, you are always consistent. You were never comfortable with her hair."

"She has too much of it and it's crinkly. Not nappy, just thick and crinkly."

"Just not straight enough for you."

"No, that's not true. Her hair is different from my sisters' or mine. My aunts and my mother and Grandma Mazzie had hair more like--"

He cut her off before she could finish, "Like white people."

"Our hair was easier to manage than Judy's. I am not ashamed to say that if it hadn't been for you I would never have let her hair grow so much, without doing something with it."

"You know something Karen, if I didn't love you so much, I would probably find you offensive, but I know you mean well and that you're doing the best you know how."

"Of course I'm doing my best. I always give my all to my family. I wish Junior and Judy would try to understand me the way you do."

"You never give them a chance. You always dispense advice and opinions in a manner that leaves little room for them to respond. Just like now, you find fault with Judy's hair, the way she styles it. But she favors the style, would it be so hard if you said something nice about it?"

"No"

"Well, tomorrow complement her, say something nice. Promise me." He turned his head to look at her and found her starring back at him, hurt in her eyes. "Promise?"

She nodded her head in assent.

Scooter turned out the lights once more, drew Karen into his arms and cradled her head on his chest. "I know you intend the best for her, I just want you to let up on her a bit." He loved her without reservation or condition. She had strange ways sometimes and even plucked his nerves on occasion, but he did not feel any different about her today than he'd felt twenty-six years ago when she first walked into his life.

Finally, the three people in the 7,000 square-foot house were asleep, but it was doubtful anyone of them was having sweet dreams.

* * *

She'd had a busy week, but found time to go with Karen in search of a special pair of shoes to wear to the cabaret. Much to her relief, Karen didn't discuss Judy, not one time. However, both of them found it hard to understand why Marva was not coming home for the dance.

"Did she tell you why it was so important to go back down there before this Saturday?"

"She wanted to be home at the same time as her sister."

"This is her third time in six weeks. I'm surprised she'd stay away from Al so long."

"I don't see anything wrong with it. Marva's just like the rest of us. She's at loose ends. The question is, what do we do now that the children are grown, the jobs are boring and we're not exactly at that special place we set out for years ago." "Still it doesn't make sense to me. Has Al said anything to you?"

"About her being out of town?"

"Well, about them?"

"Karen, please. What are you getting at?"

"She's been acting strange lately. Let me see how best to describe her. It's like she's finally decided that what she has with Al is all she's going to get?"

"And that is a mighty gift."

Rosalind W. Johnson

Chapter 6

Heleena had only missed two of these dances in the last twenty years. They were fun and relaxing and money from ticket sales went to the national alumni association. Except for a few out-of-towners they were mostly people she saw at similar functions. Even after Greg left she attended with Scooter and Karen or Al and Marva. Scooter and Al usually bought individual tables, but they always set together. They gave away the tickets they didn't use to other friends. It was the same when Greg was around.

She was excited and eagerly looked forward to the dance. Karen picked her up around four and after depositing her evening clothes and over-night bag upstairs; they talked.

She'd selected a beautiful black gown. A piece of the sensual silky fabric circled her neck and was anchored to the rest of the dress by two slim straps, one in the back and the second in the front. Her shoulders and arms were covered in the sheerest black lace. The bodice gently molded her breasts, then flowed in a swirl to just above her ankles.

Although she tended to wear unobtrusive gold jewelry, tonight she wore glittering diamond studs in her ears, two carats each. She wore no other jewelry. She'd swept her hair gently to one side and her dark brown eyes shone almost as brightly as the stones in her ears.

As she gave a final look in the mirror, the face that stared back glowed with anticipation. There was no sign of the momentary feeling of loneliness. Still she could not help thinking, it would be nice to have my own escort tonight. She'd begun to miss the intimacy that comes with sharing the cares of her days with a husband or lover. The need had an unusual grip on her these days. Friends are fine. Lord knows I couldn't live without them, but the warmth and comfort of a man's touch in the middle of the night is what I need, and soon.

Because Scooter was late returning home they were the last of the group to arrive at the dance. All of her concerns about tagging along with them evaporated when she was welcomed into the group. The only person missing was Marva. Heleena's place setting put her between Scooter and Al. She naturally turned to Al. Their close friendship and easy camaraderie were a perfect start to the evening.

He leaned close enough so that no one heard him whisper, "You look good enough to eat."

She smiled playfully and dropped her voice. "Help yourself, Dr. Harris."

Karen leaned around Scooter, "I know Marva hated to miss this dance."

"Maybe."

Everyone at the table knew each other so conversation was easy and relaxed. This same group had shared a table for years.

Even without an escort, Heleena danced as much as the others. She moved around the room, stopping for small conversations with old friends. The affair was half over when she had her first dance with the men at her table: Scooter and then Joe who sat on the other side of the table with his wife. Her first dance with Al came only after she asked him. One of her favorites was playing. He appeared unusually subdued tonight.

"I absolutely cannot sit down on this one. How about it, you and me?"

Without a word, he took her hand and led her to the dance floor. He gathered her in his arms, but before they caught the rhythm of the music someone stopped them. Cephus.

"Prince, what's happening, my man?"

"Hey, it's your world."

"No, no, you're the man to beat." After slapping Al on the back he gave Heleena a thorough once over, appreciating what he saw. "Heleena, What are you doing to yourself? If you don't stop this you'll hurt somebody."

"Oh Cephus, stop it."

"You're looking good girl. I need to send Willie Mae over to your place. She's starting to fall down on the job, spreading every day, every where."

They laughed. Cephus was always making teasing remarks about his wife, but everyone knew of his ever-growing love for her. When he walked away they drew together again and smoothly merged with the other couples, fitting together as naturally as though they belonged. She followed his lead, enjoying every minute of this closeness.

"Cephus was loud as usual, however, I can't quarrel with what he said, you look fantastic tonight."

"I accept any compliment from you because I know you're sincere."

"Whoa, Cephus is outrageous but he was damn sincere about you."

"For all the years I've known you, you've always been in my corner. Always."

He squeezed her tighter, pressing her into his chest in a way that was comforting and new. But the lights were low and the music was good, and of all the people in the world she knew he didn't mind that she was enjoying herself.

He dipped his head and softly began to sing along with the music, the words to "Unchained Melody."

Then the music stopped. Reluctantly Heleena pulled away and they slowly made their way back to the table.

Heleena danced the night away, enjoying every minute. She knew most of the people and was no threat to the wives and girlfriends. So her laughter and teasing became part of the night.

Even Scooter commented, "I don't remember you being so footloose in the old days."

"At this stage in my life I just want to have a little more fun. I refuse to do anything that lacks joy for me and I like being here with people I know and with whom I can have fun."

"You're way ahead of most of us then. The majority of the people here tonight are just marking time. Probably the only other exception is Al."

"And we all know he always runs his own show," Karen said. "But tonight he's more quiet than usual. Look at him over there with Gloria and Jimmy."

"Oh, I think he's only tired. You're right about him. He's taught me many lessons about looking at life. I don't know what I'd do without him. He is a great guy."

"I never heard you speak so passionately about Greg."

She hunched her shoulders. "What can I say? Greg is Greg and Al is Al."

"A pair of lucky guys too."

"That's a strange thing to say. But you're always giving people more credit than they probably deserve."

"Heleena you're one in a million and I'm damn grateful that you and Karen are friends."

"You'd better check with my children before you make that conclusion, but thanks for the good thoughts anyway."

As the evening came to an end, she and Karen headed for the ladies' room, stopping here and there to chat. As they moved toward their destination they missed the few envious stares and catty remarks at one table. "Two peas in a pod. I wonder where the other member of the trio is." The two whispering women laughed.

When they returned to the table only Scooter and Al remained.

"Are you ready to leave?" Al asked.

"Oh, you're taking me home?"

"Uh Huh."

"I thought I was going with them," she gestured toward Karen and Scooter who were now standing and saying good-byes to another couple.

"No, I told them I'd take you."

"Okay, let me say a few words to Gwen and Paul."

"I'll send for the car and wait for you in the lobby."

Having danced all night, Heleena immediately removed her shoes the minute she settled in the car. "It wasn't necessary for you to drive out to my house. I was prepared to stay the night at Karen and Scooter's."

"I'd planned to get you myself, but I had scheduled some business matters today and I wasn't sure I'd finish in time. So, Karen agreed to pick you up."

She did not think it odd that her friends took it upon themselves to make sure she was escorted to the social events they all attended. It was a typical of the links that bound them. *Maybe they feel sorry for me. No matter, I refuse to feel sorry for myself, tonight anyway. I had a great time.*

"Will you stop for a while, have a cup of coffee or something?" She was reluctant to let go of the good feelings tonight.

"Sure."

She looked at him, wondering why he was so quiet tonight. *Maybe he's working through a problem and is distracted.* Immediately she tried to think of something that would cheer him. It was almost 2:00 a.m. when he drove around to the side of the house to park. She stepped out of the car in her stocking feet and he reached for the black silk pumps.

Once inside, she brewed fragrant Colombian Coffee and added a tiny bit of Kenyan. As it dripped she looked over at Al who had removed his jacket, tie and loosened the top button of his shirt.

He'd turned on the TV and was looking at one of those late, late night talk shows, leaning back with his feet on the big square table. Even distracted his fine looks were undiminished. He looked up just in time to see the intense look on her face. As their eyes held she saw something in the deep brown depths she had never seen before. It frightened her. The coffee mug she held crashed to the floor, shattering around her bare feet.

"What's wrong sweetheart?" He asked as he came behind the counter.

They stooped to the floor at the same time. "Nothing. I'm probably just stressed. You know me, my stress level is always on autopilot. The cup just slipped from my hand."

He took the large broken pieces from her and set them on the counter.

"Come over here and sit down. Relax yourself."

"Let me get you another cup of coffee first. After giving him his cup she slid to the floor, at his feet; leaned back, her elbow resting on the sofa. Her legs stretched out, ankles crossed. She too, was now looking toward the TV.

"I don't know what my life would have been like all these years if I had not known you and had your friendship. Thanks for all the times you listened."

Pulling her closer he began to massage her neck and shoulders. For more comfort she slid between his knees, closed her eyes and leaned back.

"That feels good."

"You're nervous. Let it go, whatever is bothering you."

Her lips parted slightly and the strong fingers momentarily stilled. He stared at her parted lips, no longer able to hide the intense pain on his face. Stroking gently, his fingertips barely brushed the length of her graceful neck.

She let go a soft sigh.

When his lips touched hers, there was no thought of pulling away. It never crossed her mind. The feel of his lips; hard and soft at the same time, felt so natural she strained for more. He held her head with one hand increasing the pressure of his lips as his free hand slid down to stroke the rise of her breast. She felt herself drifting, but could not pull away.

The pleasure overwhelmed her. It was only when his fingers moved lower that she mustered enough will to break the spell. Breathing heavily she rose and walked to the counter, her back to him.

After a few seconds he came up behind her. Without ceremony he circled her in his arms, pulling her tight against his chest. "Sweetheart, please don't run away from me. Please."

She didn't even notice the southern drawl that had crept into his voice. I should run, run for my life. Even as this thought came to mind, the pleasure and comfort of his embrace had a stronger pull. All the longing, loneliness and need to feel the warmth of his body came rushing in on her. There was no other thought, only the sensations flooding every corner of her being. She pushed into him. His body's reaction was so sudden and violent, that for a fleeting second he felt unreasonable fear. But, the pressure of her body, mixed with the shock of his intense longing, caused his heart to pound furiously.

She warmed to the comfort of his embrace. His touch released a brush fire of emotions. "This isn't right."

He turned her so their faces were inches apart. Trembling, she opened her eyes and looked into the deep brown pupils staring back at her.

"Oh, but it is. It's us Heleena, you and me. Don't pull away from me and don't be frightened." All the while he was holding her tighter.

He is my friend. We have something special. This is ours. The waves of pleasure continued to wash over her. "I'm sorry. I didn't mean for this to happen."

Without relinquishing his grip he held her tighter, forcing her head back so that she could not avert her eyes. "Have I ever given you any reason not to trust me?"

She shook her head.

"Then don't be afraid. There is nothing you or I can do about this."

He saw a question in the depths of her eyes.

"It's the way things are between us." He pressed her head to his chest.

Her emotions took flight. She felt warm, but at the same time, fear swept through her, mingled with longing; a hunger so strong it seemed to stop her breathing. What about...? She couldn't form the words. A jumble of thoughts whirled through her mind. I have known him forever, cried on his shoulders, taken his advice and relied on him so many times; some other voice spoke to her. And now this.

Tears pooled in her eyes and one big tear rolled down her face landing on his wrist. She felt his heartbeat, causing more tears to flow. Some other emotion, shame maybe, briefly immobilized her until the longing emerged victorious.

This time as their lips met she yielded to the powerful feelings raging within her. Her lips became greedy and her world narrowed to the circle of his arms, his smell. Slowly he lifted his head: they knew there was no turning back now. Reluctantly she extracted herself, turned and made her way up the back stairs.

When he came through the dressing room, her back to him, the silk dress was falling to the floor. His breath caught in his throat. She was now wearing only the briefest of black panties as he'd imagined all evening. The little fight left in him evaporated like smoke. "Ah, baby."

When he again put his arms around her there was no doubt or resistance, only this deep longing that needed fulfilling. So this time when his arms enveloped her, she welcomed them and pressed the length of her body into his.

He had lived a lifetime waiting for this moment, to hold her, emotions unchecked. His feelings for her had never dimmed nor wavered. In his arms she was like a precious icon, one he'd coveted forever.

Heleena turned to face him, still looking for answers, then put her arms around him with the side of her face against his chest.

As he stroked the line of her jaw she thought about the other time he'd held her like this. The night she called him when she finally came to grips with Greg's leaving. Al came over and stayed with her through that miserable night. She'd clung to him. They had lain together on the couch in her study, as he'd comforted her. When she thought about it later, it was a scene right out of the ridiculous. But, he'd refused to leave until he was sure she would be okay. It was not unusual given the nature of their friendship. Except for her family, she'd always depended on friends for everything; their love, patience, understanding, companionship and now this.

He pulled away from her slightly, the tips of her breasts just touching his chest. Taking her face into his hands he lowered his lips to hers. There was no hesitation, her lips parted and she accepted his thrusting tongue.

The desire for more of him caused her to suck greedily on his tongue, which he withdrew causing a mewling sound in her throat. Al was in no hurry. He had waited more than twenty-five years.

She attempted to press her body back to his. "Wait baby, we don't have to rush," he whispered.

Arms around his neck she was now standing on the tips of her toes, her mouth locked on his. As she floated in pleasure he removed her arms, "Just a minute, let me get out of these clothes."

She watched him as he carefully undressed. He was magnificent. She had seen most of his body before, at the beach or at pool parties, but this was different. He is beautiful, all six feet four inches of him. He smiled that wicked smile of his when at last her eyes returned to his. She was frozen in place as he came toward her. Never in all the years she'd known him did his nickname fit him more aptly than now.

She moved into his arms. The next minute they were on the bed. Time stood still.

His lips closed on hers, gently at first, then demanding, almost harsh, but she welcomed it, every pressure, each thrust of his tongue. His body half covered hers as they lay locked together.

Oh God. Oh my God.

Al's mouth moved lower, now on her neck, but she wiggled down, her mouth seeking his. He raised himself on his elbows, once more holding her head still while he plundered her mouth. The tip of his tongue was everywhere at once and before she caught her breath, he took one swollen nipple between his teeth and gently tugged.

Heleena was frantic. "Al," she moaned. "Please."

She opened her eyes, passion had darkened the pupils. Her normally dark brown orbs now appeared black.

"Sweetheart, we don't need to rush, I've waited so long to hold you like this, to touch you and love you, I want us to enjoy every minute. He pushed stray hairs from her forehead, and placed a kiss there. "Don't rush me, I want to take my time loving you." He rolled onto his back taking her with him, cradling her head on his chest. Then he reached down and covered them with a sheet. He held her head with one hand and with the other, stroked her shoulder and breast.

Heleena snuggled closer, wanting her body to touch every part of him. She could feel he was ready for her. Why is he holding back?

The sensitivity of her body was heightened and the hair on his chest pricked the side of her face. As she rubbed back and forth she felt the tight little bud of his nipple. Immediately she began to lick it. Then her mouth slowly followed the line of hair down his chest.

When she reached his navel, she flicked the tip of her tongue in and out and moved on.

"Heleena. Baby, you don't know what you're doing."

She was lying on her stomach. Her mouth was warm and soft. His desire to savor this night, to prolong their pleasure was slipping away.

With all the strength he could muster, he lifted her head. She was on her knees now. When she looked up at him, her whole body suffused with passion; he almost lost the fragile hold on himself. Her hair in disarray, her nipples swollen and dark, and her parted lips made her look like some wild creature.

As he slowly raised himself she came into his arms and again touched her lips to his. He locked on hers with bruising pressure and simultaneously rolled her onto her back. He was alternately tender then demanding and his hands and mouth were everywhere. She was on fire, her nipples almost painful with the pleasure he was giving her. Heleena was sure she could stand to wait no longer, but when his mouth and tongue caressed her in the most intimate way, she cried out. "Al." Again begging him, "Please, now." But he was having none of it. His assault of pleasure continued.

He felt the tension rising in her and knew the instant she began to find her ultimate pleasure. Al quickly rose on his elbows and when he plunged into her, his mouth caught her cries. Years of longing went into every thrust.

His pent-up up feelings for her flowed like a swollen river, unending, and his body gave to her as much as he took. He made love to her now, the love he'd held back for so long. Waves and waves of pleasure swept through him, all of his extraordinary control gone in a thundering jolt. He thrust deeper and when the hot liquid began to run through her body, she again cried out her pleasure. This time he let her have her wild release.

When at last she came to herself and opened her eyes, the hunger she'd seen in him earlier had not diminished. "I love you," he said. He was still inside her and she was holding him tight, arms and legs, not wanting this intimate contact to end.

When finally they lay together with her face cradled in the curve of his neck, her body continued to tingle. Her nipples still ached for his touch. Her lips were swollen.

"I love you," he said again.

She reached up and covered his mouth with her fingers, "You don't have to say that."

"I've waited a long time to say those words to you," he said between her fingers.

"Why?"

"It's a long, long story."

They were quiet for a time. Heleena, who hadn't made love in ten years, was burning for more. At that moment she could not comprehend what Al's being in her bed meant; what led them to this situation. All she knew was she had to have him again. Soon.

Since she had no secrets from him, especially now, she had no hesitation in being vulnerable with him. "Al?"

"Yes sweetheart."

"Were we always moving to his point?" Before he could answer, she asked another question. "Did you know? Was I too dependent on you? Did I lean on you too much?"

"You know better than that."

"Why now?"

Minutes passed and he didn't answer. The only sign that he'd heard her was the tightening of his arms.

"One day I saw a girl, a beautiful girl in an elegant dress. And when she smiled at me I was transfixed, wanted to know her. Do you remember?"

"We were at Shirley Ann's wedding. The few times we ran into each other after that, never gave me time to say anything to you."

"Well, I didn't see you again until the night of the blind dates. My plan was to be your date that night. But Greg rushed in and claimed you. As they say, the rest is history. The most I could hope for was that he'd slip. Of course he never did."

When he paused, the heat from his body seemed to increase. "We were always going out together. There was never a time you and I were alone. However, when I decided Greg had no right to stand in my way, other events conspired to put a greater challenge in the way of my plans."

She knew he was referring to his hastily arranged marriage.

The night was quiet. In the dark room, only shadows moved. Years slipped away, then returned. Two hearts were beating together, but individual thoughts ran alone.

"Heleena, baby, are you falling asleep?'

"No."

"That was a difficult time for me, but what happened, happened. Our past is something we cannot change, no matter how we wish to do so." A deep sigh caused his chest to rise. "After all these years whenever I think about that twist of fate, I still feel the pain."

"Shish."

"You should have been mine Heleena."

"In a way I am. You are always here for me. My very best friend." And now my lover.

"I didn't plan tonight, but time has a way of working things out."

His hands moved with the gentleness of a lover's touch. He turned her over and proceeded to make love to her once more. When his fingers touched her she was ready for him again. He put a lifetime of lost moments into every move.

When they were quiet again, Heleena thought he was dozing. She slipped from his arms, unable to fall asleep. She started a pot of coffee in the kitchenette adjacent to her sitting room. Twenty minutes later when she returned to the bedroom with the coffee and two cups, he was awake.

"I was about to come looking for you."

"I made a pot of coffee," she said, pouring a cup for him and one for herself.

She let her robe drop to the floor and climbed back into bed. Her body was amazingly firm and tight for a woman who'd given birth to three children. The only evidence of childbirth was three small stretch marks just above her left hipbone. Her breasts were still high and firm. She was desirable and Al's eyes greedily covered every inch of her.

He took her one more time before both of them fell into deep and exhaustive sleep; Heleena still in his arms. This time her back pressed to his chest as his hand cupped one breast.

He woke her slowly, with light kisses on her neck and back. "What time is it?" She asked, stretching like a contented feline.

He nipped her on the neck. "Almost eleven. I need to get ready to leave. If I don't do it now, I won't be able to."

"Okay," she said. But, she did not feel okay. Already she was missing him and he hadn't even left the bed. "Look in the cabinet in the dressing room and you'll find extra toothbrushes and whatever else you need."

She lay, not moving until he returned fully dressed; tux, white shirt and tie hanging casually around the neck of the open collar. He set on the bed next to her and she boldly put her arms around him.

"We'll talk later," he told her.

"Whenever," was her only response.

"I want to apologize for acting like a teenager who just had his first piece."

She smiled. "Your actions were fine with me; every single one of them," she emphasized. "I have no complaints."

"Good."

She did not get up to see him to the door. She set the alarm from the console next to her bed.

Two more hours passed before she roused herself. She had been well loved and was reluctant to break the spell. I can almost pretend he is still here. His scent permeated the bed.

Whatever this means, it can't be changed now. But there was no way to stifle the most important question. What about Marva?

* * *

At one o'clock she remained upstairs. A cauldron of emotions simmered through her. Like any woman new to love, her body was alive as it had not been in years. She recalled everything that happened last night. In her mind's eye no detail was left wanting. She held each minute up for replay and joy.

The ringing phone abruptly intruded on her thoughts. She grabbed it on the first ring, but made no response.

"Heleena," the voice on the other end said.

"Karen. Hi."

"You're still in bed?"

"I am, just lazy this morning."

"It's after one."

"I know I ought to get up, but I feel the need to hug the bed today. You know how that is. Sometimes I need to lounge in bed longer than usual."

"I guess."

As Karen launched into conversation, Heleena's thoughts went back to last night. She could easily follow Karen's talk without much effort. As her friend rambled on about nothing important, she, instead, heard only intimate words spoken with a Memphis drawl, slow and excitable. He left home thirty years ago and this is the first time I have ever heard that accent so thick.

"Did Marva tell you when she's coming home?" She abruptly asked Heleena.

"What?"

"Did Marva say when she's coming back home?"

"No."

"What did Al say?"

"Just that she was staying longer than she'd originally planned."

"She didn't miss much."

"I thought we had a nice time."

"So, so. We've had better times."

Maybe you have, but for me I cannot even imagine when.

The day was nearly gone when she forced herself downstairs. Finally, the call she'd been waiting for all day came.

"Sweetheart, are you okay?"

Suddenly she felt shy and was unable to answer him.

"Heleena?"

"I'm here."

"Everything okay?"

No. If you didn't know me so well, I would say yes.

"Well?"

"There's nothing wrong--nothing at all."

"You're sure?"

"Yes I am, and you?"

"I couldn't be better, I assure you."

And last night, have you thought about last night, too?

"Remember, between us, there are no barriers, none--not anymore. Promise me you won't forget it."

"Promise."

"Listen, I can't get by tonight, but I will see you tomorrow."

She quickly bit back the word about to tumble from her lips. Why?

* * *

As she turned off the light and covered herself, only his scent shared her bed tonight. His smell was still alive in her nostrils, the special scent a man has--that musky mixture of clean sweat and the afterglow of lovemaking. She turned her head into the pillow trying as hard as she might to hold onto this much of him.

No life stirred in the big colonial out in Bethesda. The mistress of the house was down south reining in her own demons. The young girl was away from home, doing what all young girls in love do, spending time with the object of her affection. The master of the house was sitting alone in a darken room sorting through his own feelings for a woman.

He'd decided to stay away until he cooled down. She meant more to him than the physical. Even now, still ringing in his ears was the way the husky sound she made deep in her throat came with a rush when she let go her passion.

Rosalind W. Johnson

Chapter 7

"Leatha, its crazy. I've started to crave him, all the time. I just want him. I've never felt this way before. He's all I think about."

"That's only because the affair is so new."

"It's no affair."

"Whatever you want to call it, it's new."

"I've known him forever."

"Tell me about it?"

"Don't be critical"

"I'm not critical, just trying to be objective. When you called and asked me to come out here, I had the distinct impression you wanted to discuss this problem with me because I am objective?"

"That's true, but just stay neutral until you know everything."

"I'll try. But, I have to say I've never seen you like this. You are so intense."

"That's because it's the first time."

"Who else knows?"

"You're the only one. You know me Leatha I don't gossip about other people and I certainly don't tell my own personal business. I almost talked to Carolyn, but I was afraid she might not see the situation beyond my interests."

"Well, you're in an explosive situation as you damn well know. But I want to ask you one thing, something that I remember from a long time ago. It's a question that stayed in my mind for years."

"What is it?"

"When you told me why you wanted me to come, I started recalling something. Remember when I stopped here on the way to Stockholm for the first time?"

"Sure I remember."

"I went to a party with you and Greg?"

"I don't remember us going to a party together."

"Anyway, you all started playing a word game and somehow you landed in Al's lap. You were sitting in his lap, for God's sake, as though you had every right to be there."

"Sitting in his lap?"

"Yep, there you were. I found it so odd. I tell you, for a while I thought you all had gotten into that swinging shit. I really did?"

"What?"

"Heleena, you don't sit in a man's lap, with his wife and your husband there, without license to do so."

"I don't believe this."

"For years I wondered."

"Deleatha Holloway, you've known me since I was sixteen, how could you think something like that."

"It was easy. I had seen a lot of that among you upwardly mobile professional black people."

"Well you see some of everything and anything on the west coast."

"That may be true, but for a long time I thought you guy's were swingers."

"When did you decide we were not?"

"I can't recall. However, I gradually began to see that this unique relationship between you and Al was something different."

"Well, thank you."

"What I'm trying to say is that you were real comfortable with Al, and this, quote, friendship with him, is accepted by the other members of your group."

"We were always close, right from the beginning."

"Which, we, you and Al or the friendship of the entire group?"

"Well, all of us. No matter what, we've always been there for each other."

"Which brings us back to why you sent for me."

They were sitting on the patio sipping weak wine punches. Deleatha, or Leatha as everyone called her, had been Heleena's roommate their last three years in college. They'd gone their separate ways after graduation but the friendship remained, keeping in touch by phone regularly and visits every few years. Leatha had been a business major. She was now a Senior Vice President of one of the country's biggest computer firms. She'd had a brief marriage that ended in divorce. She then began a relationship that has endured for the past fifteen years.

"Well?"

"Thank you for not censuring me. I have been so discombobulated by this thing, that..."

"Wait. Stop. If you want to work through the situation, you'd better call it what it is, and stop saying, this thing. You are having sex with another woman's husband, your friend's husband, no less."

Heleena's heart skipped a beat.

"You're right of course, but you want to know something, I don't look at it that way. I guess I ought to feel guilty, but I don't."

"So, the real deal is out on the table. Now both of us can speak the truth."

"Be honest, what do you think?"

"If you weren't in such a serious predicament, it would be funny. This is so unlike you, so out of character. Maybe it's a mid-life crisis? I mean, you, roommate, the girl who wouldn't call a guy on the phone even if it meant sitting at home.

"We were just teenagers then."

"Same people though." Leatha slipped out of her shoes. "Have you thought about what it means for your future?"

"Not really. I've tried to figure out whether I saw this coming or should have."

"Well?"

"I don't think so."

"The two of you are so close, maybe deep down, for you, this was the natural extension of the friendship."

"I've thought about it from that angle too."

"Did you think back to the time you first met him?"

"Yes, even before Greg, but Al is different. He's not the same as other guys."

"Obviously."

"I examined my relationships with most of the men in my past and it's like I enjoyed them when we were together, but when they left, sometimes I felt a sense of relief."

"How did you feel about Greg?"

"I think I loved him, as best I knew how. He is really a great guy and I was hurt when he left. I remember when I realized he was truly gone, I cried most of the day. That night Al came over and stayed with me."

"And?"

"Well, we talked all night and he just held and comforted me."

"Uh, huh."

"There was nothing inappropriate. Just a friend comforting a friend. Marva knew he was here."

"Where were the kids?"

"They were with Karen."

"Go on."

"Anyway, when Greg and I married it was the natural progression of relationships in those days. Today I would never marry him."

"Hindsight is always twenty-twenty."

"True, but being as objective as I can, I have to admit we weren't right for a forever-and-ever union. Not one time in my life, have I ever saw a man I wanted and really went after him. To tell you the truth, I wouldn't know what to do."

"You're doing something. If you weren't, how could you hold a man's interest for over twenty years?"

"You don't understand, I never went after Al. We were close friends, don't you see?"

"Heleena, I'm not sure you understand what has happened here. From all I know, you sort of bound him to you. He was always picking you up from somewhere or taking you some other place. You relied on him like a husband almost."

"No, no, no. You're wrong."

"If you say so. One of your biggest problems is that you are hell-bound to see only your point of view. Now, I'm not saying it's impossible but rarely do men hang around women on a friends-only basis. I think those situations are exceptions to the general rule."

"Leatha, I sent for you so you could help me work my way through this, not for you to be accusatory. I need to get this situation clear in my mind and I want you to help me. So please try and see things from my side."

"There you go. I rest my case."

"You know what I mean."

"There's another important question I have for you, but I'll wait until we've finished our discussion. So, why was Al able to hang around so long?"

"Because he is the kind of man a woman wants to know in any capacity."

"Is that knowing in the biblical sense? Just kidding."

"You've been around him, Leatha. Who wouldn't enjoy his friendship? We just hit it off from the very beginning. I am not going to lie, I am very comfortable with him, as I have never been with any other man."

"Answer my question, be specific. What is it about him that is different from the others?"

"Let me think a minute. It's extremely difficult to be objective now, but, believe me Leatha, I'm trying."

"I know you are kiddo. Just having a little fun with you."

Minutes passed as Leatha sipped her wine.

"Well, he's bright and..."

"He's..."

"He's..."

She was struggling to find the words which would convey those special qualities about him that first drew her and still bound her to him.

"This is fascinating. And what else." They looked at each other and burst into laughter.

"Okay, so you can't be objective. Just tell me in your own prejudiced words."

"Good enough. He's a hell of a man and he cares about me. Seriously, he values my opinions."

"Hell, you're a lawyer, everybody values your opinions."

"What I mean is, he really listens to me. He's always done that. We talk together about many subjects, easy talk. We don't have to filter our conversation."

"Why do you think he wants you?"

"Because I'm the only woman he has ever been close to who doesn't need him to take care of her. Its' kind of complicated and a little hard to explain. When his father died he assumed responsibility for his mother and sister. Then Marva--you know--got pregnant, next thing he was a husband and father. Instead of being responsible for two women there were now four. His sense of responsibility just continued to move on automatic pilot."

Heleena stood, hands behind her back, still searching for the right words. "Then there was our friendship, he didn't owe me any kind of duty. I hate to keep saying this, but we were just friends, two people whose friendship grew stronger. Because he is a man who knows women, the emotional side of women, I was in turn, drawn to him. And like any friendship Leatha, it developed into something special. Over the years each of us put more into the friendship and took more out of it. He reminded me, one night, of the first words I ever said to him."

"What?"

"At his cousin's wedding, where I first saw him, he said I came up to him teasingly and said, and I quote "If you are the groom, then I'll be the bride." He said we laughed and began a conversation. Can you imagine someone remembering an initial conversation that occurred so many years ago?"

"Sure, if it strikes the right cord."

"We had almost no contact until the blind dates. I saw him one or two times in between."

Leatha waited for her to continue.

"I've been searching my memory, sometimes in the middle of the night trying to recall my impressions about him in those early days.

The only thing I can come up with is that I took his friendship to heart, like you, Karen, Marva and all my other close friends."

"Are you saying there never came a time when you leaned on him for more support than expected of a friend? Men like to feel needed."

"I told you it's complicated. There were no demands. I will admit, looking back, I always found him attractive and I believe I was special to him."

"I'm glad to hear you finally admit that much. Do the two of you talk about this whatever-you-want-to-call-it?"

"Not yet. It's only been four weeks since the relationship took a different turn. I don't know why we don't, it's strange."

"What do you talk about?"

"The subjects of our conversations have not changed. We share ideas, discuss issues that are of interest to us, sticky situations that may be happening in our work lives, things that friends talk about."

"And you don't consider your present circumstances a fair topic of discussion?"

"Probably."

"You're in an explosive situation without an escape plan."

"I don't see it like that. Our friendship is alive and well. The additional tempo is separate and apart."

"Heleena, you've started to rationalize. I think you played a significant part in this whole situation." Leatha held up her hand, cutting off Heleena's denial.

"Just wait. Let me finish. I think deep down inside, you recognized Al's attraction to you and you not only cultivated it, you encouraged it."

"What?"

"Wait, I haven't finished. I'm not letting him off the hook either. You all played a dangerous game and now you're caught in a snare of your own making. I don't think either of us can deny that Al always intended to have you in the exact position you're in now, panting after him like a dog in heat."

"Leatha, that is not fair."

"Fair or not, it's true. Listen to me girl. Now I'm going to get real common, down in the gutter. No matter what you call it, you are fucking the husband of one of your best friends, every chance you get."

"That's low."

"Yes it is. You know we've come so far, we tend to forget some of the basics in life. Look at you, big time lawyer, assets coming out of the yang yang; a spectacular home, friends to die for, everything you could possibly want, but they do not change, one iota, the fact that you are sleeping with someone else's man. Can you deny it?"

Heleena was suffused with heat and began to sweat. But Leatha would not let up.

"It's not my intention to be mean or hard, but I think you have to admit the truth. You didn't send for me to be a yes-man. I could have stayed in Seattle and listened to all this by phone. I thought what you wanted from me was an honest assessment of the latest development in your relationship with Al."

"You're right. We've never been anything but frank with each other. But you make it sound so vulgar, like something nasty. It isn't."

"I'm sorry, that's the way you see it, but even if I used less graphic words, your actions are still the same."

"I call it making love."

"I say having sex."

"With a friend."

"With a married man."

"No matter how you describe it, it is more than just sex."

"You can't seem to tell me what it is. All you can say is what it is not."

"It's wonderful, Leatha. Having shared so much with him over the years, and now, to have him in the most beautiful, most intimate way is almost beyond description."

"Now tell me about the good stuff between you and Dr. Harris."

"I can't tell you everything, girl, but he is good, magnificent. We never rush."

"Uh, huh. Go on."

"It's hard for me to believe he is 53 years old. If he is this good at fifty-three, he must have been awesome in his twenties. I couldn't have handled it. No way."

"Shut up."

"You know Leatha, I could only discuss this kind of shit with you. But when we're together we make love at least three times. I know a lot of women whose husbands or whatever, younger than 53 can't perform like that."

"This is wild."

"Now don't laugh when I say this but I, want to make love just as much as he does."

"I'll be damn. I won't be able to look at him straight again, without wondering. "Hey, Al can you go four times or maybe five?"

They hollered.

"Oh, he can, believe me. He's tender, thoughtful and extremely passionate. My reaction to him is totally different from Greg."

"How?"

"With Al I'm more open, and more--."

"Aggressive."

"Definitely, more aggressive. He knows I want him every time, as much as he wants me."

"And that wasn't the case with Greg?"

"Not to the extent it is with Al. With Al, I get a little wild."

"Shut up, girl."

"Oh yes, don't you ever feel like that about Doug?"

"Doug and I are like old shoes. We're very comfortable with each other and we have great sex."

"Then you understand."

"I understand the love a woman has for a particular man. You may find it hard to believe from our conversation, but I also understand how that same love can take on a life of its own."

"Thank you. I don't hop into bed with him every time I see him."

"We've been close a long time. I would never criticize you. I just don't want you to forget the real problem."

"Leatha, you know I understand the serious situation I'm in. And I know he and I will have to talk about it soon."

"Will I see Al during my visit?"

"Sure. He'll stop by here."

"This is one for the books."

"I keep trying to tell you, nothing has changed. Sometimes I drop by his office, if he's available, and we have lunch or he'll call my office and we'll have lunch on that end. And of course, he stops by here like he's always done."

"What about Marva?"

"I haven't seen her as much as usual this summer. She's back and forth between here and Tuskegee.

"Do you think she suspects?"

"Of course not."

"Next question, do you think your excitement level is so high because you haven't been with a man for such a long time?"

"Nope."

"I don't know. When you've had a long dry spell, it can be a powerful thing to start up again."

"No Leatha, it's the man himself."

"Just an extension of your unique friendship huh?"

"Yes. I don't know if I should be afraid or what. My feelings right now can best be described as eager. There are deeper feelings, Leatha that I don't explore with anyone at this point. I'm afraid to even acknowledge them to myself."

"I sure don't envy you. You and Al have taken a big leap. I wonder what he ultimately wants from you? What do you want from him? Will you be able to socialize with Marva like nothing's happen?"

"Yes."

"You seem to take this new turn in the relationship for granted, like it's your right. When Marva finds out, you will lose your other friends."

"Which friends?"

"Karen, Billie, Carolyn, and the rest of that bunch."

"I've never been involved in anything like this before, so I don't have a survival plan. He comes over here just like he's been doing for years. Now, he stays longer and we...." She waved her hand in the air.

"Go on, say it."

"We sleep together. You satisfied?"

"Whether I'm satisfied is not the issue. The important point is that you be honest with yourself. Can you be content to live your life as the other woman?"

"I am not the other woman. Can't you see, we're the same people? We've just taken our friendship to a new level."

"Whatever level you're on Heleena, you can't stay there forever. You haven't thought this business through. I am telling you. The first thing you'd better decide is what you're going to do or say when Marva finds out. This is not like you. You're a lawyer. There might be legal implications. Marva might go berserk and come after you."

"No, no, no. Marva wouldn't do that."

"If you feel Al is such a prize and you're not even married to him, how do you think his wife feels about the possibility of losing him or even sharing him? Women have been known to get a little rowdy when they find out their husbands are creeping around."

"Marva isn't the rowdy type, believe me."

"What about your children. What's your game plan when they hear about it? How will they feel about Uncle Al then?"

"You know Leatha, we've been sitting here talking for over two hours and I don't think you really understood what I have been saying to you."

"Tell me again in one sentence."

"Okay. Al and I are friends. We have been friends a long, long time. Close friends, very close friends and I don't expect that to change, ever. We've introduced a new dimension into the relationship, that is all. I can't make it more simple."

"But, it isn't that simple to explain your emotions."

"Of course my feelings are deeper now. There is a part of him that belongs to me now."

"That sounds ominous."

"So, now do you understand my emotional dilemma?"

"Yes."

"I realize all of the questions you asked needed to be asked, it's just because I'm in an emotional whirlwind right now, and I don't want the realities to diminish what we share."

"I believe you and can only guess what you're going through. But, please promise me you'll sort through this situation."

"I will."

"We've been talking about this problem for a while and I know it's painful for you, but I need to ask one more question. Have you considered or even thought about the possibility of stopping this affair before it goes any further?"

"No. I couldn't now, even if I tried."

Rosalind W. Johnson

Chapter 8

The soft click let Heleena know someone was trying to get through to her. "I'll call you back later," she told Karen."

"Hello."

"Hey girl."

"When are you going back to Tuskegee?"

"I'm flying out tonight. I wanted to stay until Monday. But, I'm sick and tired of trying to referee this fight between Al and Selena."

"He's put his foot down?"

"I'll say and right into a pile of shit. Everybody knows she's just like him. She does what she wants to do. He never had a problem with that before because what she wanted didn't clash with his ideas of how things should be."

"Has he talked to her boyfriend?"

"Has he talked? You know Al. He's made his disapproval clear. But Selena, is determined to move in with him."

"You think she'll go ahead?"

Rosalind W. Johnson

"I don't know and I don't care. Let him contend with it. What are you doing this afternoon? I need to run out to the mall and return a dress. You feel like riding with me?"

"Sure. What time?"

"I'm ready. I'll come by and pick you up in twenty minutes."

Finding decent parking at Tyson's on a Saturday afternoon is always tough, but today they rode around for ten minutes trying to get close to one of the entrances.

"Is there a big sale here today?"

"I don't know, but it is just too humid to have to walk from the far end of the parking lot. I'll drive around one more time. Let me know if you see a spot before I do."

"Those people over there," she pointed, "Follow them. They look like they're heading toward that second row."

Marva quickly drove over to where two women were approaching a blue van. "Bingo."

Once they were inside the mall, Heleena decided she'd buy a colorful belt. It was silly to come all the way out here and buy nothing.

"Meet me over in the aisle behind the last rack of scarves," she told Marva.

"This won't take long, I'm not getting anything else, just returning this dress and taking it off my charge.

Soon, however, they were seriously going from store to store, buying nothing, just looking, trying a belt or scarf or gold jewelry, having fun. Every store had a sale, twenty to forty percent off everything.

"This is like old times." Heleena said. "By now we'd have spent three hundred dollars, remember?"

"I sure do," Marva replied wistfully. "Sometimes I think back to when we were just starting to make money. That feeling I got, just to be able to walk into a store and buy anything I wanted."

"It was fun."

"Do you ever miss the old days?" She asked suddenly?

"You mean, spending money like water?"

"Well, just that time in our lives. We didn't have any problems, we were happier, we could live life on our own terms."

"They were good times, but it was a struggle for me, the kids, career, Greg, then the divorce. I agree with you to a point. Most of us were living our dreams."

"What happened?"

"I ask myself that question all the time."

"Do you notice now when we go places everybody's kind of sighing with relief that they've made another day? People have erected protective walls around themselves. Even old friends don't seem as warm anymore. I saw Paula Greene at the grocery store about a month ago; I went up to her and asked about the children and Andrew. She seemed reluctant to talk to me. And finally she said, see you later, and just walked off."

"I guess you don't know she and Andrew are separated?"

"She must have thought I was trying to get into her business."

"Probably."

"How long has it been?"

"Just before Christmas. I saw him and he told me."

"Was it another women?"

"I don't think so. He said their marriage wasn't working and he tried to leave several times, but she pleaded with him to stay."

"See what I mean? What happened to the good times? Every other couple I know is breaking up, after twenty, twenty-five years together. It seems strange. You'd think when people have weathered so many years of good and bad, they'd be happy to hang on to the end."

"When the spark that holds two people together dies, I'm not sure you can revive it."

"Still at this stage we should be comfortable with each other, and not have to worry about coming home one day and finding a husband has taken off."

"You sure don't have to worry about that."

"Don't be so sure."

Surprised, Heleena turned away. "Why don't we find a table in the eating plaza and get something cool to drink?" She walked away toward the food area, before Marva answered.

When they were seated, each with a small salad, Marva let out a long sigh for the second time today.

"I've missed you and Karen lately, our endless talks about everything under the sun."

"I do too. Karen and I still talk everyday, but now she only whines, mostly about Judy."

"What's Judy up to now, wearing her hair in the wrong style, dresses too long, no make-up, or some other silly thing Karen finds inappropriate?"

"It's more serious this time. She's in a heavy relationship with some guy who Karen believes has a bad influence on her."

"In Karen's eyes anything Judy has ever been interested in, is bad for her. So what else is new?"

"This time she may be right."

"You know I love her as much as you do, but I can't handle her problems this summer. Between Al and Selena's battles, I don't need to hear about Karen's endless problems with Judy."

"Admittedly, it's trying, but she doesn't have anyone else to talk to about her."

"I guess. She has always laid more on you than she did on me."

"That's the truth."

After a few forkfuls of the salad, Marva switched subjects. "I'm thinking about leaving my job."

"To do what?"

"Nothing. I'm talking about retirement."

"You're kidding?"

"Oh, no I'm dead serious. I'm sick of the whole mess. Whatever joy I once felt going to work is gone."

"I almost feel the same way."

"You? You're the last person I expect to be fed up with her career."

"It's true. I'm just going on at this point because it is expected. People wonder, who leaves that kind of money?"

"Hey, good question."

"The money's not the important issue in my life now. I'm in a different phase. You're heard me say that before."

"But you rarely ever complain about anything."

"And I'm not complaining now. It's just that I didn't expect to feel, at this point, that I've missed something in my life."

"For God's sake, what?"

"It's complicated, but I feel a sense of loss as if I've been cheated out of something important."

"What have you of all people, been cheated out of?"

"Don't laugh."

"How can I? My own life isn't a bed of roses right now. Go on."

"That old cliché' about the grass being greener on the other side of the fence is certainly true of us?"

"True. I have no money problems, but I don't have a man of my own to share this life."

"And me, I have all the money I need and a man at home, and that's another story, and I'm still missing out on something."

"Exactly my point. I can count on one hand the number of people I know who can honestly say they are where they planned to be in their personal and professional lives."

"It's a shame too."

"You've been away so much this summer we haven't had the chance to get together like this just to talk. I miss that, I really do.

Marva looked at her watch, "We have to leave in a few minutes. There are one or two things I need to do before I leave for the airport."

As they stepped outside, the oppressive July heat and high humidity were smothering.

"Girl, this heat is worse than in Alabama."

"You haven't been away so much you've forgotten what Washington summers are like."

"No, but I can never get accustomed to it."

"And it doesn't get better anytime soon."

After checking herself in the mirror, Marva began rummaging through her bag looking for lipstick. One thing about Marva, she never let her guard down when it came to her looks. She was cute and she knew it and looked good in her clothes. She always wore her hair cut short, saying it made her look taller. The older she got, the shorter she cut it.

They hardly breathed until the car cooled. As a convertible passed them only to be stopped by the next light, Marva remarked, "Can you believe people still sit with the sun beaming down on their heads in this heat?"

99

"Hah, those white girls want deep tans. They want to look like us, I guess.

"In thirty years those two will look like pieces of leather. Brown leather at that."

They laughed together. When the light changed the red convertible shot ahead and was soon lost in the sea of cars around Tyson's.

"What time does your plane leave?"

"Seven ten."

"When do you get to Montgomery?"

"I'm flying into Birmingham."

"Why? Isn't Montgomery more convenient to Tuskegee?"

"Yes, but I'm staying in Birmingham tonight. I'll go down to Tuskegee in the morning."

Abruptly she changed the subject, "Guess who I saw last week?"

"Who"

"Lisa Clarke. I hadn't seen her in years."

"Remember how she would say Lester didn't want her to lose one ounce from those hips. Now she looks like a camel from the rear."

Traffic began to slow to a crawl just as they approached the bridge.

"So, how's your mother?"

"She's doing fine now. Two weeks ago I had to have all the locks on the doors leading outside changed and locks put on all the windows too. Someone tried to break into the house. I talked to her about a security system, but she refused."

"Good strong locks on the doors and windows ought to work down there."

"I sure hope so. I don't need any additional headaches, Al and Selena are getting on my last nerve with their constant arguments."

"That will stop soon, either she'll move or she won't. If she does, then Al will be forced to accept the fact. And he will."

"You're right. Then there's Al himself, his work keeps him busy. We don't do many things together anymore."

"That's life with everybody we know."

Marva seemed not to have heard her because she kept talking. "The strange thing is, I have this feeling that neither one of us cares. It's like we need this time apart."

"What do you mean?"

"Just that we probably need to spend time away from each other. It's a feeling I have. Did you ever sense that with Greg?"

"Of course. You know, it didn't take Greg and I too many years before we realized ours was not a match made in Heaven."

"That statement covers fifty percent of the couples we know."

"And it's a shame too."

"Most of those who are still married would not marry each other today."

"Probably not."

"So many of our friends' marriages are in trouble I sometimes question why people still go through with it. Secretly, that's why I support Selena's desire to move in with her boyfriend."

"You do?"

"Yes. I haven't said so to her, though, and would not dare say it to Al. I just let them have it out, but being away helps."

Heleena was burning to ask the obvious. Don't you want to be here with your husband? Instead she brought up the demise of yet another couple they knew. "In case you didn't know, Jenine and Nathaniel have separated. She started running around."

"I heard when he found out, and they started throwing mud, he justified his own activities by telling her she knew his habit when she married him."

"He does have a point. When we marry these men, we tend to gloss over the things about them we don't find so appealing, but as the years go by, one by one those old faults just rise up and grab us by the ass."

My mother used to tell my Aunt Emoline all the time about my uncle. When Aunt Emoline complained about Uncle Jacob not working, Mama said, "He's always had your behind in a sling."

"He ran around on her?"

"No, that wasn't the problem, he was lazy, never could keep a job. Mama said when Emoline met him he was out of work. The longest he's ever kept a job was for three straight months during the first year of their marriage. The only reason he had that job was because my Aunt's brother got him on where he worked.

"Uh, uh, uh."

"During my own marriage, I never thought Greg really, really wanted me. You know, the way a man ought to want a woman for his wife. It was like he was trying to take me out of circulation."

"What do you mean?"

"It's just an impression I have."

"Well, if Al and I were going together, today, I'm sure I couldn't get him to the alter."

Heleena didn't comment, she knew that was an accurate assessment of their situation. Today men don't marry women just because the bundle of joy is in the oven before the ring is on the finger.

"It's almost twenty after three. I hope this heavy traffic doesn't cause problems making your flight."

"No. I have plenty of time. I need to get two dresses from the cleaners and pack my cosmetics. I can stop at the cleaners before I drop you off."

"Why don't you go straight home after you pick up the dresses. Selena can drive me home."

"Don't count on Selena being at home. She'll be avoiding Al. She knows he'll be home earlier than usual today to get me to the airport on time."

"He's still working on Saturdays."

"Heleena, you know Al. He wants everything in his world to function according to his rules. He promised to limit the number of patients he sees. Did he do it? No. Now, every Saturday he's in that office, sometimes all day."

"He needs to be on top of everything. I don't have to tell you every Tom, Dick, and Harry is laying low, waiting to file a malpractice suit. Keeping up with all the paperwork is important."

"Sure. I can't argue the point, but I assumed we'd have more time together by now."

"Maybe in another month or so, you can persuade him to keep his word."

"Me? Are you kidding? When have I ever been able to persuade Al to do anything? Why do you think I am just as content to spend so much time in Alabama?"

"To be with your mother, I thought."

"True, but if Al didn't spend so much time at the office, I'd rather be at home."

In her mind, Heleena began to reel off the times she'd been with Al this summer. That day we drove down to Virginia, the day after Leatha left, the second weekend this month..."

"Hey," Marva reached over and touched her, "you just did it again."

"What?"

"Shut down on me, just drifted off. What were you thinking about?"

"Nothing important."

"If I didn't know you so well, I'd be miffed."

"Too many things on my mind."

"When you said you were feeling restless you really meant it didn't you?"

"Oh yes."

"A couple of months ago when you first said that to me, I didn't understand what you meant, now I think I do. I have some of those same feelings myself."

"We're getting older. The minutiae that motivated us twenty years ago are not that important anymore."

"You want a man to love and care for you. Me, I want--well, I want something I don't have."

"What?"

"I'm still mulling it over. Needless to say, what I want is just as formidable as your wanting a man of your own."

"Sad isn't it," Heleena commented, as a beautiful brown face, bold dark eyes and a thin mustache over perfect lips captured her inner vision. Simultaneously a dull headache started.

Heleena turned her head. She was uncomfortable with the turn of the conversation. Two women, one man. It was a hitch as old as time, wife and lover. But in our situation I am not the proverbial lover, she corrected herself. He and I are friends, the best. I don't want to take anything from Marva. She has Al; I have a small part of him, what happened, happened. I didn't set out to seduce him. Our time together cannot possibly hurt her.

"You're doing it again."

"Sorry, just thinking how much I miss the old days, all of us being there for each other, all the time."

"Me too, looks like we're going in different directions."

"That's for sure, backwards."

"But, backwards may not be so bad, if it gives us a chance to start over."

"What would you do differently?"

"Go back home right out of law school."

"But you were already busy up here and married."

"That too might be different."

Oh shit. Sounds as if she's trying to say something and I don't want to know what it is. This is the third time today she's spiked the home front.

"We're so busy talking, you missed your turn."

"No I didn't. I have time to take you home first, we can talk a while longer."

When she drove up the driveway and stopped under the portico, Marva turned off the engine and lowered the windows. "When I get back in a couple of weeks, we'll get together, Karen too, and spend all day doing nothing serious, just having fun and a lot of girl talk."

Heleena reached over and hugged her tightly, "Take care of yourself and don't worry about Selena, she was always able to handle herself in most situations."

"Oh, I'm not worried about her. Her beef is with her father."

"He'll come around to her point of view. You'll see."

"I don't think you understand kiddo, it doesn't matter to me, one way or another."

Heleena quickly hugged her again, and got out of the car. Once in the house, she stepped out of her shoes and left them in the foyer. She walked down into the huge living room and picked up one of the small Ibeges from its nook. The fine old patina of the wood gleamed a deep reddish brown. She ran her index finger across the face of the little statue. The sacrificial marks on both sides of its face stood out in relief. She put him back and sat on one of the four sofas surrounding the large square slab of marble.

Ten minutes later, still restless she walked about the open room touching the five-foot high tree-of-life configuration then the traditional Makonde female figure with the lip plug. She lovingly stroked the curves and planes of the heavy ebony pieces.

When she wandered into the loggia she stopped and picked up the silver framed photo of five young people taken more than six years ago, the last time they'd all been down to Hilton Head together. They were all smiles in casual beach attire. Johnny in swim trunks and shirt, Richie, shorts and no top, and Anne, two-piece bikini; Selena and Judy were similarly attired. They were beautiful girls, smiling the flirty smiles as only pretty young girls can.

Setting the frame back in its place Heleena just sat, staring out at the patio. By nightfall she'd started reading three books, discarding each in turn. A funky mood had taken hold. She thought back to the afternoon with Marva. I miss her, and the old Karen, too.

This kind of moodiness was rare for her and she was having difficulty pulling herself out of it. In a final act of desperation to calm herself, Heleena took a long warm bath with exotic oil. By ten o'clock she felt refreshed and somewhat relaxed, but avoided going to bed, and put on a pair of soft white cotton pants with a pale blue tee shirt. Without make up and in her bare feet she was back downstairs when the side doorbell rang. It could be only one person.

When she opened the door and saw his smiling lips, she rushed into his arms, breathing his scent. His arms closed around her, squeezing tightly. Now she felt comforted, warm, and secure. She lifted her mouth to his.

Rosalind W. Johnson

Chapter 9

A typical south Florida morning, at eight o'clock the temperature was already above 80 degrees. Judy and Arieta had just pulled onto 95 at 79th Street. Peter's family lived closer to 83rd, but Judy had taken a liking to mangoes and a little store off 79th Street had them. They'd gone by the store to buy a bag to bring with them.

She was so pleased all the family welcomed her. They'd had a chance to get to know her, because there was no place for her to hide in a house where twelve to fifteen people lived at any given time.

Happiness showed in her face. "What are you smiling about?" Arieta asked in her lilting West Indian accent.

"I had a wonderful time down here. Everyone was so pleasant to me. What about other members of your family, are they always so open to strangers?"

"They're a loud group. There are so many of us, sometimes it's hard to tell who belongs and who doesn't."

Arieta was like the rest of her family, talking constantly, and loud too, so unlike my own family. "You all are so happy together."

"Yes. What did Peter say about us?"

"Nothing specific."

"You mean he doesn't mention us?"

Unlike her mother, Judy was not practiced in the ways of guile so she answered truthfully. "Sometimes, but the only reference he makes is, my family will do this or I can count on them to do that. When he made arrangements for me to come down here to drive back with you, I was reluctant."

"Why?"

"Because I didn't know you. When I said this to him, he only said, you don't need to know them, you know me."

"We have always stood for him, everybody in the family. He expects us to do anything he asks. Grandma Tina spoiled him. Whenever she had a little something extra, she 'd only spend it on him. He knew he had this pride of place with her, but he never took advantage."

"What do you mean?"

"You know how when some people are spoiled they let you know they can have their way. But Peter was never like that. It was his manner that made us always bow down to his wishes. We are so accustomed to doing his bidding that we would never think to be displeased with someone he favors. So when he said you were coming we were excited. You are the first woman he sent home to meet us."

"You don't have to tell me that. I don't care about other women in his past."

"That is a good thing too."

As they rolled north the heat and humidity settled in the car like heavy vapor. The old beat up station wagon had working air conditioning once. However, it was long dead by the time Arieta and her family came to own it.

Arieta's natural exuberance was a perfect foil for Judy's reserve and the two of them hit it off famously, first time they met.

Arieta doted on her two children who were now playing together on the back seat. Children had a prominent place in this family, Judy noticed. Everybody loved them. She'd had so much fun with all the family and really looked forward to the next two days with them. By

Wednesday, they would have dropped her off and be on their final leg of the trip to New York.

Judy wondered about the children's father who she hadn't met. Arieta rarely mentioned him, although the children sometimes referred to him. He was a long distance truck driver, they said.

"You and Peter, things going real good huh? You feel much for him?"

"Oh, yes."

"I can tell. The way you say his name, your face lights up, you shine. It's good, huh?"

The look on Judy's face was the only answer she needed.

"Maybe next time he will come with you."

"Are you inviting me back?"

"Of course, anytime."

"Somehow I can't picture Peter with so many people."

"Well, he likes time alone, but he blends in. When he's had enough of all of us, he leaves. The children love him to come because he brings presents for them."

"How is he with the children?"

"What you mean?"

"Does he like children, like having them around?"

"I don't know, but he is patient with them. Why?" Abruptly she reached across the seat and put her hand on Judy's stomach. "Is something there?"

"Oh. I just wondered, coming from a family with so many children. I never heard him say one way or another."

"Mama will we see Uncle Peter tomorrow?" Came a bright voice from the back seat.

"No, the next day."

"Will he give us presents?"

"Why you think you always get presents? No, we bring him presents."

Four hours later she was still behind the wheel. The children were napping on the back seat, their little heads close together and Arieta still talking non-stop. Judy drifted in and out of the conversation. She had no trouble staying awake. The excitement of her visit was still new and she was eager to get back to Peter.

"I'll relieve you at the next rest stop."

"Okay, my knee is getting tried."

Judy's braid had started to come loose and the humidity was playing havoc with the long thick tendrils. As was her way, she felt no concern for what her mother called her wild urchin look.

"You and your brother, are you close?" Arieta asked

"We were."

"You're not anymore?"

"In a way I guess we still are, but he doesn't live at home now. He moved away."

"Where?"

"Out west."

"Don't you miss him?"

"When he first left I did, now I've grown accustomed to being by myself. He always stood up for me when he lived at home."

"Stood up for you? How?"

"Whenever my parents were on my back, at least when my mom was on my back."

"You and your mama, you fight?"

"No. There has to be two people for a fight. With my mother you either give in or prepare for her to go on and on."

"So, you must agree with everything she says to get along, huh?"

"Not only agree, but do whatever she asks?"

As the miles rolled behind them, Arieta and Judy cemented their friendship, sharing secrets in the manner of women.

The blazing late afternoon sun was in its last gasp and the heat in the car, stifling. The little party was sweaty and tired. Cars were on the road from every state and Canada. When Arieta took her turn at the wheel Judy began a game with the children, trying to guess the states by the color of the license plates. Later they sang songs together.

Finally, when the others fell asleep, Judy's thoughts found free rein. The highway was level and straight with few distractions. The wagon's motor was holding its own so far. Arieta's two brothers had worked on it all day Saturday to make sure it did not cause problems for them on the trip. They even took it down to a friend's shop on Sunday to make sure all parts were in good working order. They put four brand new tires on the car.

I hope we can continue our friendship. Judy looked over at Arieta, whose head leaned against the side of her window. She seems to like me. It's hard to believe that not one of them criticized my hair, they actually liked it. Mommie would have a fit if she knew I was down here wearing my hair braided. Peter said it was the thing he noticed most when he first saw me. A beautiful smile crossed her face as she pictured him, his hands cupping her scalp then moving slowly through to the tips, straining to touch every strand. I miss him so much. I wish mommie would just see him for what he is and not as some person who is not good enough for me.

"I'd better start looking for a place for us to spend the night. Peter made me promise we would stop at dusk and not try to drive at night."

"You ready for me to take over?" Arieta asked, through a long yawn.

"No, I just need you to help me look for a place to stop."

"Why don't we drive into Georgia?" I'm rested now. I could do about three hours."

"No, Peter said we should stop before its too dark. I don't want him to worry."

"Worry? Peter? How can he worry, he doesn't know when we stop."

"I want to do what he says. I promised I'd call him by a certain time."

"But you said Thursday after he called you that you could not reach him at that number again."

"I did, but he gave me another number to call him tonight. He wants to know we're okay."

"What's all the secrecy for? We drive until we get there. Don't you want to hurry and get there, then be with him?"

"Yes, but I promised."

"Okay, we look for a nice place, but not too expensive."

"Peter told me to find a place near the highway."

"You mind everything he say, huh?"

"Well, he has a lot of experience."

"There are motel signs everywhere, let's try the next one."

They were near Jacksonville and the wagon hadn't given them any trouble. Judy was surprised at its performance given the beat-up exterior. Having ridden in expensive foreign cars all her life, she'd just naturally expected something fancier for the road. Good at masking her true feelings, she'd hidden her skepticism whether the car could make eleven hundred miles. "Quality Inn, 2 miles from exit," Arieta said, pointing to the sign.

"Let's try that one."

As Judy took the exit, Arieta reached into her bra and withdrew a wad of bills, peeled off several and replaced the remainder securely in its hiding place.

"One Hundred Dollars should be enough for one night and to fill the tank and get some food."

"Oh, don't worry about it, I'm paying."

"Your Peter wired money to pay for everything."

"No, you keep the money. You can have a little extra to spend in New York. I'll charge everything."

"You sure, its okay?"

"Yes, put the money away."

Without further argument Arieta replaced the bills with the rest of her stash.

* * *

Peter was sitting in the dark room leaning back in the chair with his long legs resting on the sagging bed. He'd been smoking herb all evening and the scent was heavy in the room. Even alone in this seedy room, in total darkness he refused to acknowledge the nagging worries about the women's progress. *Judy will call. She knows to do just as I told her, but, she should have called by now. They understood there was to be no night driving.* Without realizing it he crossed and uncrossed his arm over his chest, rocking on the back legs of the chair.

He'd been in the room since four and no one knew he was there. Earlier, he'd called his Aunt and was assured Judy and Arieta had left as planned and the car was in top shape.

Repeatedly running his hand over his face he kept thinking *she should have called by now. It is almost eight o'clock.*

When the phone finally rang, the front legs of the chair crashed to the floor. He reached for the receiver, but waited for a second ring before answering.

"Yes?"

"Peter. It's me," Judy said, happily.

"I told you to stop at dusk."

"It hasn't been long since the sun set. We got a little behind because of all the stops to feed the kids and take them to the restrooms."

"But it's after light now. I don't want you on the road at night. I mean that Judy."

"We're okay Peter."

"Okay isn't good enough. I wanted you to drive through Georgia and South Carolina between 10--3 in the afternoon."

"I know what you said, but what difference does it make? The car..."

"What's wrong with the car?" He cut her off.

"Nothing's wrong with the car. I was just saying the car is doing fine, that's why you don't need to worry about us."

"Judy don't tell me what to do."

Fretfully, she pleaded with him, "Please Peter don't be angry."

"Then do what I tell you."

"I've always done that." She tried to hide the hurt she felt.

"How are the children?" He asked abruptly, sensing her distress.

"They were fine all day, but after we checked in we discovered little Neal had a fever. That's one reason I didn't call you as soon as we settled in our room. I had to go back out to find some Tylenol for him."

"You be careful."

"I will."

"And don't forget, no speeding and fill up when the tank is half full."

"I miss you," she whispered.

"And you know I miss you. But I don't like reminding you of the importance of following my orders."

"I am, it's just that there were so many stops with Neal and Tetra as I told you, I had to go out and buy medicine." She began to plead for him to understand. "I just couldn't call as soon as we checked in, please don't sound angry."

"I hear everything you said, but its more important for you to call at the time I expect to hear from you. I may not be here to take your call at a later time, you act like you don't understand that."

Two big tears dropped from her eyes. Arieta's heart went out to her. When Judy hung up she said, "Our men, they don't always understand. We do for them, sometimes they say thanks, sometimes they just take for granted."

"When he gets in that mood, nothing I say pleases him." She rummaged through her bag, found a wide-tooth comb and began combing the tangled strands of her hair.

Without anything further Arieta went into the bathroom to give her a few private minutes. Before closing the door she looked over at the children asleep in one of the twin beds.

Neal fretted the whole night through, tossing and turning. His temperature remained steady at 101 degrees. Even though she knew Peter wanted them to move out at daybreak, the little boy was still quite hot.

"Why don't you give him another dose of Tylenol, we need to get his temperature down before we leave here," she told Arieta.

At ten o'clock Neal began to sweat. "Mommie, mommie," he called to Arieta.

"I'm here."

"I'm wet all over mommie."

"That's good," she said, feeling his forehead. "Let me take your temperature." She began to peel away his wet pajamas. When he was naked she wiped his entire body and dressed him in dry clothes.

Judy handed her the thermometer, "Check him now."

Thermometer firmly set between tongue and bottom lip he looked up at her, waiting.

Within seconds, his mother smiled. "He's fine now. His temperature is back to normal."

His sister was also standing by waiting for good news. "Can we eat now, mommie?" She asked.

"Yes. We pack our things in the car and go to McDonald's."

Judy felt relieved. Within twenty minutes they'd checked out of the motel and were headed toward the restaurant.

Finally, Judy wheeled the wagon onto Interstate 95. Arieta sat in the back with the children, one leaning on each side of her. The mood of the little party was more subdued today than yesterday.

The trees and other roadside scenery became one long blur as Judy pushed the car hard. She was in a hurry to get back to Peter.

She'd felt the sting of his displeasure last night and vowed to make up the time they'd lost this morning.

"Watch the speed signs, why you driving so fast?"

"I'm sorry," Judy said.

"You don't have to be sorry. We don't need ticket, though." She knew Peter had upset her greatly. From the moment she hung up the phone, after talking to him, Judy was anxious and agitated. She'd had a frightened look on her face all morning. When she left the room to go down to the desk to pay the bill, Tetra asked her mother, "What's the matter with Aunt Judy, mommie?"

"She can't wait to get home."

Peter told her to avoid the stretch of 95 between the intersection of 26 and just outside Florence. He'd explained police were stopping blacks and harassing them, claiming they were looking for drugs. He told her to take highway 26 to Orangeburg, then to get on 601 to Interstate 20 then to 77 until it runs into 85; from there she was told to stay on 85 until it merged with 95 at Petersburg.

He had been adamant on this point. Even last night she had to repeat the instructions just as he'd written them.

She was nearing Orangeburg, but because they'd left so late, she wanted to make up the time lost due to Neal's fever.

"He made me promise to leave 95 at Orangeburg, but I don't know, we lost so much time already, I just want to hurry and get there."

"Peter?"

"Yes."

"You better do what he say. He knows these things, better than you. Let me drive a while. You rush too much now, drive to fast. You too nervous."

"I just don't want to make him angry."

"He's happy, you do what he tells you. This is the way they always come. My cousin Brinny say always be careful to leave 95 at Orangeburg, so they know."

Three miles later she pulled into the rest stop and got out of the car.

"I need to use the restroom quickly," she said and made a beeline for the building. As she rushed to make it, she held her stomach. As soon as she squeezed through the door of the first cubicle, the retching started and everything in her stomach came up. She was sweating profusely as her stomach heaved two more times. Holding onto both sides of the cubicle she pushed herself up, trying to catch her breath.

When she'd calmed herself, she sat on the seat holding her head up with difficulty. Ten minutes later she returned to the car. The heat in South Carolina was no less oppressive than in South Florida. She sat in the car while Arieta took the children into the restroom.

As the hours wore on, they wilted from the heat build-up in the car. The children became more irritable. To give Arieta a rest and a chance to sit with the now belligerent children, Judy took the wheel again around five, just sixty miles south of Tenneco County, South Carolina, Jim Crow territory.

The man in charge of Tenneco County, Sheriff Tommy Lee McHickey, did not provide safe passage for drug pushers, at any price. He accepted a few gratuities here and there, but never from those who would use his roads for the transportation of drugs. His baby brother had died in the gutter in New York City after being hooked while flirting with the mess in college. He'd been the first member of the family to ever go beyond high school.

* * *

"This is our chance to move into bigger distribution. I planned it this way. Three trips before, and everything worked to plan. Fourth time will go same way. Judy know to stay with route, she will follow my instructions."

Both of them were smoking weed and the room stank of it. Ansel noticed Peter was chain-smoking the drug, had been since yesterday. This was unlike him. He wondered why, but didn't ask.

"This good stuff, where you get it?" Ansel asked.

"Same place." Peter was distracted, many things on his mind. His thoughts took flight. Maybe I came down too hard on her last night. Everything should work like clock.

As he'd done all his life, Ansel watched his cousin closely, waiting to do his bidding.

"When this deal goes down, you think we can take time to go home?"

"No. We move now, bigger things. No more petty deals. We move more fire power too, more money."

"But," he started to ask, why. Peter cut him off immediately.

"We move or we die, man. In this business you never stand still. These cats are too violent. They settle differences like animals."

* * *

"Slow down," Arieta said from the back seat. "It's getting dark," she'd been watching Judy and her driving was becoming more and more erratic. She was no longer talking, just driving, rushing to get back to Peter.

"We need to make up the time we lost."

"Peter, he's going nowhere. When we get to Baltimore, he'll be satisfied. Don't worry so."

"But you don't know him when he gets angry with me."

"I know him good and well. Let him stew for a while."

Judy slowed, but began to pick up speed again, thirty minutes later.

"Let me drive for a couple of hours and you sit back here with the children."

"I'm okay, anyway they'd rather have you with them."

It was not long before she'd again exceeded the speed limit about the same time as the light rain started. Arieta's eyes were fixed on the back of Judy's head. That braid of hers had come loose again. Her hair seemed to swell in the heat and humidity.

It's a shame such beautiful hair and she cares nothing about it. So busy was she watching Judy she didn't notice they'd gone into a series of curves and a small sign that called for reduced speed. Neither of them saw the policeman sitting casually behind the steering wheel of his cruiser parked on the shoulder protected by the rain and misty fog slowly rising from the ground.

They weaved pass him doing 30 miles per hour above the posted speed limit. He silently pulled out behind them, and the first thing to catch his eye after the excessive speed was the Florida tag.

* * *

Three a.m., and she still couldn't get to sleep. Heleena had been staring at the ceiling for two hours. She shifted all four pillows behind her back and sat up in the bed. Only the moon lit the darkness. Across the room, Mr. Wilson stared back at her, black as coal; eyes unblinking; scorn clear in his face.

"This is one night I don't need your disapproval," she said out loud as she rose from the bed, walked over to the statue and turned it around to face the glass wall.

Back in bed, she settled into the pillows again. Why should I beat up myself? I didn't pursue this part of the relationship with him. Contrary to what Leatha said, it just happened. "But is it right?" the little voice questioned.

It is not a question of right or wrong. He is my friend. She threw off the sheet covering her lower body. This bed is no place to think. She walked to the window and stood looking out into the night. A tableau of pictures clicked in her head, all in black and white; no colors to blur the intense contrasts. And Al in every one of them.

Such a slim figure standing dwarfed by the huge panels of glass, she'd shed about seven pounds in the last month. Even he noticed it. He'd commented on how much lighter she felt in his arms. Hugging her elbows, she finally walked to the phone, sat on the floor, her back to the bed, and dialed.

Three thousand miles away Leatha answered, "Hello."

"Hi, it's me, Heleena."

"Well, well, well, so, what's up?"

"Same old number."

"I've been expecting you to call. What took you so long?"

"What do you mean?"

"Your situation is one that requires plenty of discussion, even if you think everything is hunky-dory."

"I need you to be serious now."

"I'm always serious. How are things going with you and the Prince?"

Heleena ignored the emphasis Leatha placed on his nickname. "Our relationship is stronger than ever."

"Whoa, and of course cemented by the strongest of glue. Look girl, I'm just having a little fun with you. Something is bothering you or you wouldn't call me at three thirty in the morning."

Leatha's caustic remarks didn't bother her, but tonight she needed words of comfort. "I just need to talk. I can't sleep."

"Is everything going okay? Strike that. Are you and Al still...?" She left the remainder of the sentence hanging.

"Yes, we're still in the same posture."

"Can I take that statement literally?"

"Please Leatha."

"Sorry."

"You know this whole thing is a first for me and I'm not sure of the rules."

"Are you having second thoughts?"

"No, and that is what worries me. I'm happy with things as they are. Does that make me some kind of bitch or hussy, or some other loose floozy?"

"No, just the other woman."

"I'm the same Heleena I've always been."

"What is it you want to talk about this morning?"

"I don't know, I truly don't. I just wanted to hear a friendly voice."

"I hear something else behind your words. You sound worried."

"I'm not worried. I'm nervous and restless. I can't sleep."

"So this call has nothing to do with Al."

"This call is about me. Al and I are what we always were, very, very, close, I just need to have a more realistic line on where I'm going in this part of my life with him."

"And of course you have to figure in Al's part in the scenario." Leatha waited for her response, she knew Heleena was dodging the real issue, but she'd wait for her to get to the point. "You haven't called all this way in the middle of the night just to share girl talk."

"For some reason you want me to put myself into compartments, my friendship with Al in one compartment, cut away from the rest of me. How can you expect me to do that?"

Leatha waited.

"He is a part of the whole fabric of my life."

Leatha's snort came through loud and clear.

"What is the plan Heleena? Do you and Al have a roadmap to where you're going? Do you have a plan for next month, next year, the future?"

"No."

"You'd better be warned then, relationships don't flourish in a vacuum. They ebb or flow; evolve, develop or whatever you want to call it, but for sure they don't stand still." Now she asked the question that she knew Heleena had not asked herself.

"Where do you and Al plan this elevated relationship to go?"

"We don't think about that."

"You mean you don't talk about it."

"We don't need to talk about the future."

"Cut the bullshit Heleena. This is me you're talking to. And you know I see through all that shit. Why the hell did you call me if you don't want the truth." She plowed on, her annoyance growing.

"Your ass now wants more of Al. And no matter what you say to me, I know for sure you are worried about what his plans are."

She paused for a minute.

"You're not even sure if Al is serious or if he is just playing?"

"That's a nasty thing to say."

"Oh no. That is the only question to ask. And I know deep down you have wondered, is he just playing with you because its easy. Every woman alive, once she begins to pine after a man, wants to know his position. You're no different. Although you always considered yourself somewhat above ordinary human vices, you are just another woman with all the vulnerabilities that every woman has in her relationship with her man. But in your case, with somebody else's man."

"You're predictable if nothing else. I don't need a tirade."

"Excuse me."

"What would you do if you were in my predicament?"

"Number one, I would be honest with myself by really coming to grips with what I want from the relationship."

"What would you expect?"

"I would expect to love this man, unconditionally. I would expect to receive the same kind of feelings from him. My desire to spend time with him would run unchecked. And I can tell you I would resist any feelings of guilt. Be honest, how do you see the future with Al?"

"Whether you believe me or not, I haven't really thought about a future. To me, our relationship is like a circle which has just closed."

"What are you talking about?"

"I told you what we have is a natural extension of our long and close friendship."

"Come again?"

"Just what I said, we've gone into this with eyes wide open and we are happy with it."

Leatha didn't know what to say. After two minutes of silence, Heleena continued.

"I'm not planning for the future and I won't let the future take him away from me."

"And Marva? What about Marva?"

"This has nothing to do with Marva."

"Heleena, you are slipping. Your situation has everything to do with Marva. What is your rationalization for saying otherwise?" Her voice began to rise again. "How have you reached this conclusion? How? Please tell me?"

"You don't have to scream."

"I'm not screaming. I'm annoyed at this convoluted way you've started to think about your involvement with another woman's husband."

"Please Leatha. We're talking about Al. A man who has been close to me for twenty-five years. He's been more than a friend. A kind of love has always existed between us. He knows everything about me. Whenever I needed him he was there. No questions asked. The fact that he has given me the ultimate expression of his love does not change that. And because I give it back to him, I can't feel it's wrong."

Leatha could feel her struggling to reach the conclusion she'd already made.

"I hear what you're saying, but I don't understand it. Are you saying you have a right to this ultimate expression of love?"

"Yes. I feel I have a right to all of his love, every bit of it."

"Regardless of Marva?"

"How many times do I have to tell you, this has nothing to do with her. Over the years, Al and I have created a unique relationship."

"I'm trying to understand, really I am. You and Al have a cozy friendship, which started out platonic, but is now sexual. He has a wife, but you're satisfied with what you have, and you don't expect her to object to it?" Her voice went up an octave, laced with incredulousness. "Is that what you're saying?"

"What I'm saying is that..., well, she doesn't know about it and it isn't necessary for us to be.... Frankly we don't spend anymore time together than we ever did."

"Is he now running by your place for a quickie or are you stopping by his office for one?"

"You don't have to be vulgar."

"I'm not being vulgar, but if you two are not spending any additional time together, then how have you closed the so-called circle?"

"Just take my word for the truth."

"Why did you call me then? I take it Al is with Marva tonight?"

"He isn't here of course."

"There's something bothering you and I can tell you don't recognize the real issue yet. You can call me anytime. Okay?"

"Thanks."

"Remember, I don't judge."

"I know. Bye Bye." She replaced the receiver, dejected. She and Leatha did not connect this time.

After making a cup of coffee, she moved slowly down the back stairs and out onto the inside patio. Gradually, her thoughts returned to her friend's probing questions.

I have to believe it was meant to be. I am not trying to break up his marriage, this is separate, and I'm not looking to take him from Marva. Her head began to ache. For once I have a problem I can't discuss with the one person who knows everything about me. Do I have the right to share in his love?

The ringing of the phone intruded on her solitary deliberations. Unhurriedly she went into the kitchen, not at all curious about who could be calling at the crack of dawn. But before she could speak Leatha rushed to apologize in her own special way. "Sorry. Let's start again."

"What"

"I wasn't very comforting two hours ago."

"You're always straight up about everything."

"I couldn't get back to sleep knowing you were troubled and I wasn't very sympathetic. I apologize."

"Accepted"

"The two of you have been like hand and glove for a long time. Maybe the physical thing was inevitable. Who the hell knows how these things happen, anyway. I do have an opinion, however, on what could come of this, a broken heart, yours, and worst of all the loss of a life-long friendship or two. Be careful and accept the fact that what the two of you have now, is probably all you ever will have together. That's all I have to say."

"I appreciate your frankness, but I can honestly say I don't expect Al to leave Marva."

"I really believe you are convinced you don't need to have Al all to yourself. Well, be careful anyway," she insisted. "Go on and get some sleep. At our age we can't afford to face the world with haggy faces."

"You too, take care of yourself. Love you."

Is Leatha right, am I deceiving myself? Maybe, maybe not. She went back upstairs and climbed into bed.

* * *

Thirty miles away another person had spent a long sleepless night, anxiously waiting. Once again Peter sat in the corner of the dark room. The air was thick with the aroma of herb. Ansel had returned and sat silently on the bed leaning over elbows on his knees, with his head resting in his hands. Accurately gauging Peter's mood, he said nothing, just waited for directions.

He'd been waiting with his cousin since early yesterday, more than twenty-four hours. But they'd heard nothing from Judy and Arieta, who were to have arrived in Baltimore Thursday night. When they didn't, Peter had allowed for unexpected contingencies, so Friday morning they looked for them to arrive at least by noon.

Now it was Saturday morning and still no sign of the women and children. His cousin was beside himself. Because he trusted Peter in all things, Ansel didn't worry. Peter knew what to do. So while Peter stared forward though a haze of smoke, Ansel just sat not daring to break the quiet.

Peter sent him on two errands last night and he was proud, he'd performed as directed. He'd also been sent out to call Miami to see if they'd heard from the women. But, no, they'd heard nothing.

123

Judy always did what Peter told her to do, so why she had not arrived by now, Ansel couldn't fathom. He did not venture to speculate about their tardiness, either.

* * *

It was early afternoon when Heleena roused herself. Six hours of sleep had cleared her headache. She was also feeling better about her late night talks with Leatha. A quick shower and she was ready to face another day.

She called Karen to check on Judy. "Have you heard anything from her yet?"

"No. I guess there's no need to worry. She said she'd be gone for a couple of weeks. I don't want to start calling down there. If she isn't home by Monday, I'll track her down."

Chapter 10

She experienced her first uneasy moment after agreeing to go to the club with Marva.

Rich's Place was a carryover from their school days. Back then; Georgia Avenue was peppered with small intimate clubs where they sat and listened to jazz, pop and almost any type of music. Now Rich's was the only one left.

The club was not as smoky as it used to be, but those who smoked didn't worry about someone asking them to put out a cigarette. They came here to relax and for some puffing on a cigarette helped. So a cloud of smoke drifted above the tables, but not thick enough to cause discomfort.

Rich's catered to 40-60 year-old black professionals. They could eat good food, and feel safe. They moved in an alien white world all day, but here they shed the tough protective outer demeanor and socialized in their own way. It was open every night except Sunday and Monday. On occasions like tonight, they even heard some of the good old music, live. Usually those old tunes could be heard from the restored Wurlitzer, sitting prominently near the small raised dance floor. The music varied, sometimes jazz, pop, oldies, just good music. Tonight the club featured 60's music.

"Remember that club down on Randolph?"

"Ellie's"

"Uh huh, that was my favorite."

"Why? It was always so crowded in there. You could hardly breathe."

"Because it was so intimate. I would practically have to sit on Al's lap. He wasn't crazy about it, but he went along to please me."

"You sure had a plan to catch him."

"I did. I wanted him so I had to plan ways for us to be together."

"And it worked."

"But, its something you have to constantly do. I still have to plan hard for us to spend time together. When Selena was younger, it was easy. Al agreed to anything if it involved her. Now it's tougher."

"You sound like you have to force yourself on him."

"Staying married is harder than getting married. You should know that."

Heleena was relieved to hear the group tuning their instruments. She was uncomfortable with the direction of conversation, but a little curious too.

The guys were still great together. Al alternated with Hosea on the piano, Crim on drums, and Lloyd Monteith on sax. They all sang. After so many years, they still got together to jam. And sounded damn good. They played together here at least two weekend nights per month and were usually joined by Rich's girlfriend, Shirley. It was fun and relaxing for them. Al and Crim were physicians, Hosea worked for the federal government and Lloyd was a high school science teacher.

The performance was fun for the group and the audience. Al and Shirley were the only members of the group with any formal music training. Al had taken piano lessons as a kid. In his high school band he'd been trained to play the sax, the trumpet and the trombone. During his military years, he had had the good fortune of traveling around with a band entertaining the troops.

When Rich took up with Shirley, she was singing professionally. Everyone teased her about giving up the possibility of making it in the big time. Other local people had done it, Donnie Hathaway and Roberta Flack. She always responded, "Love is more important." Although they never married, Rich lived with her in a house he'd bought for her and put in her name, only. "It is her house," he corrected anyone who presumed otherwise.

"I still can't understand why Shirley didn't give herself the chance to make it in the music world. She is so good." Marva said, clapping her hands.

"What she has with Rich is more important. They have an enviable relationship."

"According to whom?"

"Look at them Marva. He has never even looked at another woman. They've been together forever."

"True."

Heleena could not see her face clearly, the lights were low and they were sitting side-by-side facing the area where the performers stood.

"But you sound skeptical. Do you know something, I don't?" She asked, looking at Marva's profile, "About them?"

"No. I just don't know if it's a good idea to give up the possibility of an outstanding professional career for the uncertainty of love, even marriage."

"It has to do with what is important."

"You didn't give up your career for hearth and home."

"It wasn't an issue for me or Greg."

"The issue probably doesn't come up for most couples. I sometimes think maybe we put entirely too much emphasis on the importance of relationships." She was now looking directly in Heleena's eyes.

Heleena held her breath and thankfully the music started again. This time a duet between Shirley and Crim, "Ain't No Mountain High Enough, Ain't No Valley Low Enough."

Al sang the next song, "Could This Be Magic." Heleena put her hands in her lap and tried to make her face blank. She had learned with great effort, to calm herself when she felt a stress headache starting, but it wasn't working now. The furious pounding of her heart made her thankful for the low light. The words of the song floated around her, like a caress. Her eyes fixed to the side of the stage, she sat perfectly still, not daring to move.

Maybe I shouldn't have come tonight. In the pit of her stomach a deep hollowness settled like lead. The urge to run was almost too much to bear. The music stopped and she let go her breath. It came out as a sigh.

"You okay?" Marva asked, frowning in the dark.

"Uh huh, small headache."

As Al left the stage and walked toward their table, the butterflies in her stomach stirred, but she couldn't turn away. Someone at one of the tables stopped him, but two minutes later he was seated between them.

The minute he sat down she felt the heat emanating from his body. Crossing and uncrossing her legs under the table, she held her hands clasped in her lap. When his arm innocently brushed hers she jumped. Thankfully it went unnoticed.

"Shirley is still good. Every time I hear her, I can't believe she gave up a chance to make records," Marva told him.

"She made her choice. Years ago, a person who wanted to make it in music had to leave here, go to New York, Detroit, Memphis, or some other place, and she just wasn't willing to make the move."

"I know you're right, but it's a shame anyway."

Heleena drew into herself, mentally pulling away from his nearness.

"You guys are good enough to go on the road," Marva said.

"Think so?"

"Oh, yes."

"It would have been fun years ago. We're too old now."

He turned to Heleena. "I know we did a couple of your favorites, so why are you so quiet?"

"Anytime I hear you, well, the group," she corrected herself, "I can hardly believe you're only performing for fun."

"That's all. I couldn't pay for the relaxation it gives me. I'm taking requests for the second round. What do you want?"

"That's easy, "You Don't Know Me."

"And I want Shirley to sing "Me and the one I Love," just the way Dinah Washington did it," Marva said.

"Good as done."

Heleena struggled for normalcy. Although she'd been to this club many times, tonight was almost laughable. Al could be singing to either one of them and her emotional capacity to remain aloof was seriously eroding. While he sat between them, like always, as if nothing had changed, Heleena's emotions churned wildly.

Her head began to ache.

"You're so quiet tonight. Is anything wrong?" Al asked leaning closer to her. Before she could answer Marva chimed in, leaning forward looking around Al, "I asked her the same question."

"No, there's nothing wrong. I have a mild headache, that's all."

Al pushed his chair from the table, turned to face her and held her head between his hands, his eyes piercing her to the core. "Tell the truth, are you okay?"

At his touch, her chest began to heave and all she could think about was the closeness of those beautiful lips that she longed for even now. "Yes, I am fine, just a headache. I'll take a couple of aspirin and that should get rid of it."

Satisfied, he let her go and turned his chair back to the table.

Pull yourself together girl, you're acting like an infatuated teenager.

Fumbling in her purse she found the bottle of aspirin.

"Let me get you a glass of orange juice to take those with." He called to the guy behind the bar, who came immediately "We need a glass of orange juice, Jim."

In the last month these headaches had begun to plague her. She was sure it was because of stress caused by this business with Al.

"Intermission's over, I'll see you two in thirty minutes."

Before he left the table, Heleena and Marva gave their parting requests. "Do a Marvin Gaye song," Marva reminded him.

"Tell Shirley don't forget "I Cried a Tear"", Heleena said.

Back together on stage, the group discussed their next set. Then the good stuff started again. The satisfied "oohs and ahs" floated across the darkened room.

"Did Al say anything to you about Selena?"

She didn't know what to say, afraid Marva might suspect something and was trying to trap her. "No. Why?"

"She's still pressing the issue about moving in with her boyfriend and I think she spent a couple of nights at his apartment while I was away."

"I thought he'd put an end to that discussion."

"You heard me. The last time she brought it up he went airborne, berserk, crazy. He's spoiled her rotten, so now the chickens have come home to roost."

"Ah, Marva, she's not spoiled. Selena's a wonderful child."

"What do you call a child who had three different cars in high school?"

"A privileged kid."

"No. I call her spoiled. We all know how he has given into her every whim all her life."

"Marva, he's good to all the women in his life." She almost bit her tongue, but the words were out before she could stop them.

"True. I can't argue with that."

"But, Selena has always been his pride and joy. Just like any other father, he can't deal with her growing into womanhood."

"Fathers easily imagine some guy doing with their daughters, what they once did with another man's daughter."

"Tell me about it, Greg is the same way about Anne."

"Heleena, you remember, Al was a fast mover himself."

Heleena looked at her sideways. "How would I know that?" She was beginning to feel flushed and knew it was not menopausal.

Marva pulled her arm and looked directly into her eyes. "Now I wasn't exactly a blushing bride and you know it."

Noncommittal, Heleena hunched her shoulders just as Shirley squeezed through the tables and sat beside them. Heleena breathed a sigh of relief. Maria Brown followed her to their table.

"Marva, your husband is making me sweat. Girl he is good, I mean real good", Shirley said.

"I have to admit you're right."

"How're you two doing?"

"I'm fine." Heleena said. "And you Maria, what have you been up to? I haven't seen you for a while?"

"Just working and trying to get away from those kids. That's why we're here tonight. Gerald's back home. He and Marian are fighting like cats and dogs, something they never did as children."

"You've got your hands full girl." Marva said.

"Carlos and I had the house to ourselves for almost two years, before Marian came back home. When she did we thought it would be for a short period of time. It's been a year and a half and she shows no signs of leaving, now Gerald's returned."

"It's happening everywhere. If Rich hadn't bought that condo for Beverly she'd still be living with us."

Shirley looked at Heleena. "How do you keep your children from moving back home?"

"Just lucky or maybe it's because I tell them constantly that I'm thinking of selling the house and buying something smaller."

"Are you?"

"I've given it some thought, but nothing definite. But you know Shirley, when you've been a single parent, that time is doubled. It's like being sentenced to ten years in jail, but serving twenty."

They laughed.

"I can tell you Carlos is not happy. He's eligible for early retirement and is seriously thinking about taking it, but with both of our children back home, he's rethinking the idea. We go out every Friday and Saturday now, just to get a few peaceable hours."

"Maybe you should thank your children," Marva said.

"For what? For junking up the house, having the phone ring all night, for coming in at all hours, disturbing our sleep?"

"No, for forcing the two of you to spend time having fun again. It would be nice if Al and I went out together more often."

"Well, we are enjoying ourselves just being together again. When we go to bed we now lock our room door. You know what it reminds me of? When we were young and had to sneak around to do the things we wanted to do. Only now, instead of our parents we have to sneak on our children. Hell of a deal."

"Just be glad they didn't bring anyone else with them. A woman who works with me had her daughter come back last year. She'd gone away to college, Johnson C. Smith, and had one more year to graduation. Well, she took up with some guy from down there, got pregnant and had a baby. She and the boy moved in with his family. That lasted two months, before she and the baby were back home with her mother. Shortly after she returned, guess who else came?"

"Her boyfriend?" Marva asked.

"Yes. She's back with baby, baby's dad and not a single job between them."

Heleena was trying to follow the conversation while also listening to the music, especially when Al began to sing.

"It's epidemic child."

"I can't imagine their not wanting to be on their own. When we left home there was never any thought of moving back," Heleena rejoined the conversation.

"Even if we wanted to, we couldn't," Maria said. "My father ruled with an iron hand. When he sent us off to college, he told us to take advantage of the opportunity. He said it was more than he had and if we didn't want to make something of ourselves then we could go to the tobacco fields. He paid our college expenses by the year after reviewing our grades. If the grades weren't what he expected, then he would reduce the amount he paid. Every penny we made that summer had to go toward making up the difference."

"The first time I met him, I knew he was a hard man," Marva said.

"Yes he was. But looking back, he made us independent. When I think of how he would make us get out of bed by seven every morning, I laugh. In my father's house you didn't lounge around in bed after the sun was up, unless you were sick."

"And the good thing about that was your mom didn't have to worry about a thing."

"No she didn't. But we always thought she put him up to some of his actions."

"Why don't you and Carlos start putting the pressure on them like your dad did?" Marva asked her. "I bet they'd he out of there in a flash."

"It's too late for that."

They turned their attention back to the group. Hosea was now singing "What Does It Take to Win Your Love For Me." Al was using the tambourine this time and effortlessly enjoying every minute of it.

After Maria returned to her table, Heleena again retreated into herself internalizing the words of the song, making her remember time's past. When Al began to sing Ray Charles' "I'll Take Care Of You," despair and longing mingled together so intensely she could barely remain seated.

This is ludicrous, both of us sitting here, and each believing his words are personal.

"Ray Charles has nothing on my husband," Marva said.

Heleena just stared straight ahead.

"You're so quiet, are you thinking about, Greg?"

"Don't be silly," she snapped.

"Excuse me. You've been drifting off all night. I just thought you may have been thinking about when you and Greg...?"

"My head's pounding. I need more aspirin. I'm going to the ladies room, be right back," she said pushing her chair from the table.

Once inside the tiny room she locked the door and leaned against the wall. "Get it together," she told herself rubbing her forehead. Someone knocked and tried the door handle.

"Just a minute."

Two minutes later, again in control of her emotions, she returned to the table.

"Here are the aspirin," Marva said, pushing the bottle toward her hand peering at her strangely.

"Thanks. The ventilation is not good in here."

Heleena was uncomfortable. She was mentally thrashing around for a topic of conversation to take her mind off thoughts that ought to hold feelings of guilt. "Did you talk to your mom about moving into a smaller house?"

"No. She's been in that house most of her life and the memories of my father hold her there more than anything else."

"Is that woman you hired still there to help her?"

"Yes. She's almost mama's age, but dependable. I'm going back down there next weekend. My sister and I decided we would alternate two-week periods for the next month. It's easy for me, I have so much leave and Al really doesn't need me these days. I saw quite a few of my high school classmates, even the guy who took me to the senior prom."

"Wow. He still lives there?"

"No. He lives in Birmingham, but his family lives there, so he's back and forth."

"When I go home I never see my high school classmates. But I don't go home as much as you do."

Marva turned and saw someone she recognized. She lowered her voice but continued to stare. "Hey, isn't that Juanita?"

Heleena peered through the dim light, "Juanita Green?"

"Yes."

"It looks like her, but that guy she's with is definitely not her husband, Joe."

"I wonder who he is. You think Juanita's tipping out?"

"Now Marva, don't make anything out of this, Juanita's in business, he's probably a client or something."

"Or something."

"You ought to stop that."

"I think she's up to no good."

"What if she is, it's not your business nor mine. And frankly, I don't care one way or the other."

"Well I do." With that pronouncement she stood.

"I don't believe you're going over to their table to see who that man is?"

"Oh yes I am, be right back."

Chapter 11

They sat silently in the close dark waiting area. Through the wide opening they could see a pitiful bunch of humanity behind the tough security screen. This was no place for a child raised in the most beautiful pink and white room ever, with a private bath including a Jacuzzi.

Sorting through the chain of circumstances, that led her here occupied Heleena's thoughts. They had not been allowed to see Judy yet. The lawyer was still inside the office talking with the people in charge. He hadn't even been allowed in to see her. All they knew was that drugs were found in the car she was driving.

"I didn't want her to go down there. I knew it was no good. That bastard, Peter, had something to do with this. I know he did." Karen started crying again. She'd been calm on the plane, but the minute they arrived, she became hysterical. A junior associate met them and drove them to the attorney's office. The airport was an hour's drive from Dover.

He seemed a serious and competent attorney and the top criminal lawyer in the area, so they'd been advised. He was a past president of the local bar association, which was a good sign. His standing in the legal community would be the only thing to get her out today and on a plane back to Maryland. Relying on his own position in the closed rural area, rather than seek a judicial order to get Judy out, he'd gone directly to the Sheriff. His representation cost a small fortune.

They'd been waiting two hours. The room was hot and stuffy and the cracked and stained plastic chairs, added to their discomfort.

The other people in the room openly stared at them wondering about the nature of the business that brought them to this corner of hell.

The door from the Sheriff's office opened and all eyes looked up expectantly as a draft of cold air entered the room. A tall straggly haired woman in a purple pantsuit called out, "John Thomas, come in heah." A black man in worn overalls stood immediately and went forward, stopping two feet in front of the woman, "Yes mamm?"

Without ceremony, Purple Suit continued in the same loud voice, "It's gonna cost you Seven Hundred and Fifty Dollars, cash only, you got it?"

"Yes mamm." He reached in his pocket and pulled out some money. He wet his thumb with the tip of his tongue and began counting out bills, placing each one in her out-stretched hand.

When he'd finished, without another word, she retreated behind the closed door, but he remained standing, waiting for directions. Approximately ten minutes later Purple Suit came out again and announced, "You can go to the side gate and Joe'll be released there."

"Thank you mamm."

This scenario continued until she and Karen were the only ones left in the room.

Karen fretted. This waiting without knowing what was happening beyond the closed door, began to gnaw on Heleena too. She knew in matters like this, in a place like this, money was the only thing that would free Judy. The question was how much. She'd let the lawyer know to include any miscellaneous expenses he might need to affect her release. She was sure he understood. Now sitting so long without any explanation, she too, began to worry. Was it enough?

Momentarily the door swung open again. This time the lawyer came out and walked over to them. He dragged a chair in front of them, sat down, and then smiled.

"You can go around and talk to her, while they process her out."

Heleena breathed a sigh of relief.

Back outside, the sun baked the graveled perimeter of the compound. Barbed wire prison fences loomed on both sides of them. Even in the 90°F heat, Heleena felt a chill.

When they rounded the back of the building she stopped suddenly. Directly in front of them stood two gray block buildings separated by another high barbed wire fence.

"Oh boy," she breathed heavily.

The men were housed on one side of the fence and the women on the other. There was no grass inside these compounds. The wretched human population of women was clearly visible as they milled around the yard in small groups of twos and threes.

At the small guardhouse they were directed to an area between the guardhouse and the outer perimeter fence. This area, too, was protected by strong steel wire. There were several picnic-type tables and benches. The sweating guard pointed them to the far tables.

The attorney waited in the guardhouse with the officer. They heard him call out, "Bring that new girl out heah."

Heleena and Karen slid onto the bench facing the common yard area. "All of these women, locked up like animals, everyone of them black. Well almost everyone." She noticed two fair-haired women standing near the back corner of the fence.

As they sat down, briefly, all eyes stared at them. Then everyone went back to her conversations.

"Where are the men?" Karen wanted to know.

"Probably out working -- doing road work."

"This is so dismal. I just can't believe my baby is in this place."

Heleena squeezed her forearm. "She'll be out soon. Don't worry."

"I still don't understand why that lawyer didn't want Scooter to come."

"We talked about this, remember?"

"I know, but I still don't understand."

Heleena gave her arm another comforting squeeze. These people down here don't give a damn about you or Judy or Scooter. Civil

Rights to them is a joke. For Scooter to show up here would have given these bastards a chance to slap him in the face. They would like to show him the power they have over him through his child, to jerk these uppity niggers around.

"They have the upper hand and they won't let you forget it. We don't need to have your husband subjected to the treatment these people can mete out. You paid what amounts to a ransom. Part of that money you paid will end up in the Sheriff's pocket and probably the pockets of these guards. In a place like this, the inmates are subjected to anything the people in charge want to dish out. You can't imagine nor would I want you to even try."

A huge heavy-set black woman led Judy out into the bright light. The attorney stood waiting for her as they entered the guardhouse. He walked with her toward where they sat. Karen jumped from her seat and ran toward them, crying, arms outstretched. She grabbed Judy, hugging and kissing her, sobbing continuously.

All eyes in the yard turned once more to the scene being played out in front of them. The attorney whispered something to her, and walked with them to the table. Heleena hugged Judy tightly, then moved away so she could speak quietly with him.

They stood next to the far side of the perimeter with their backs to the compound.

"We will be able to take her home with us, won't we?"

"Oh yes. They're preparing the papers now."

He'd promised them that part of the fee was a sort of bail money, but she still wanted assurance that when they left Judy would be with them. What would come later had not been discussed.

"Whether this case goes to trial depends to a large extent, on Sheriff McHickey's discretion. I'll do my best to convince him that she didn't know what was in the car, that neither woman did."

She knew the game; more money could go a long way in persuading the Sheriff to drop the matter. "Maybe he will levy some kind of fine?"

"Maybe."

"I have authorization to pay the fine."

"Good."

"What about the other woman?"

"They put her and the kids on a bus back to Florida, one-way ticket. Of course if charges are dropped against your God-daughter, the county must be reimbursed for their tickets."

"I understand."

"Mrs. Walton, I'm sorry you all had to go through this, but you made a wise choice to handle things as I suggested. The citizens of this county are unforgiving types. They would like nothing better than to make an example of the girl. You and I know what the result could be -- so I don't need to paint a picture -- if you get my meaning."

"No you don't. We appreciate everything you've done and if you will arrange for no more than the payment of a fine to close the case, we will be eternally grateful. Just tell us as quickly as you can."

"You bet."

Heleena hoped for a more definite answer, but she was satisfied a price would be set, Scooter would pay it, and they would never have to return to this God-forsaken place. He had given her authorization to withdraw up to $70,000 from an account he'd specially set up to pay this blood price. She was comfortable knowing the so-called fine would be covered.

"I'll be in with the Sheriff. As soon as her papers are ready, I'll get you all to the airport."

She remained standing by the fence after he walked away, joining Karen and Judy only after she was sure they'd had sufficient private time.

Judy was like a wounded dog. Her eyes were wild, hair tangled and the sour smell, so unreal. The heat was oppressive, but there was nothing to do but wait.

When the lawyer finally sent word that Judy should prepare to leave, they requested permission to assist her in changing clothes. They'd brought a clean dress, underwear and sandals. They were allowed into an inner area of the women's quarters. It apparently served as a common area. Even in the intense heat, there were six or seven women sitting around.

They went to a far corner and with as much privacy and dignity as they could muster, changed her clothes.

Heleena, who was always sensitive to smells, could not ignore the overwhelming smell of human misery. No amount of disinfectant could wash it away. Her nostrils flared and she began to identify odors. Unwashed flesh. The unmistaken odor of sanitary napkins worn too long. The smell of the women who were not particular about hygiene, even before they arrived here. That odor was pungent and sour. And of course, the smell of fear.

Judy's bedroom suite was itself 1200 square feet. How can this be?

"Birds of a feather flock together. You lay down with dogs, you get up with fleas." Her grandmother's voice sounded across the years.

She'd given the lawyer five cashier's checks. He'd told her to make them out to The Sheriff's Fund to Fight Crime.

Fifteen minutes later they were back on the road, heading for the airport. Heleena would not feel comfortable until they were airborne. The lawyer had finally assured her that a sum, yet to be determined, would bring an end to this nightmare.

As she looked at Judy and watched Karen trying to pull her out of the trance, a knot squeezed her heart. She could not help thinking about the past and remembering the pretty little girl, with long ringlets around her face. The pain was terrifying because it could so easily be Anne, but for the grace of God. Wrong place, wrong time. Nobody is immune.

When a man comes into a woman's life, he doesn't ask permission, he just drifts in like a beautiful old fashion summer day. The time is so right. No matter the age, the effect is always the same. He brings her joy. Or madness. It could go either way. And this child had no protection.

That scoundrel Peter had come to Judy during a low point in her young life. She was searching for someone to show her tenderness, that she mattered. Understanding maybe. Kindness? Love?

At the airport, Heleena sat across from Judy and Karen, observing them closely, as though through a microscope. Judy's nervous habit of twisting the bracelets around her wrist was the only motion she made.

That day she'd come to see me and I promised I would help. Could I have stopped these events?

During the sixty-mile drive to the airport, Judy hardly uttered a word. Now that they were almost home, maybe she would come to life and at least talk to them. Karen had pulled her hair back and braided it.

Heleena explained to them that Judy would not have to come back -- that all they wanted was money. Karen understood, but Judy showed no emotion.

The only time she seemed to come to life was when she asked about Arieta and the children. She seemed satisfied to hear they'd returned to Florida.

"I'll call them when I get home," was all she'd said.

They began the descent into National. Being so near home, Heleena could now open the door to another compartment of her life, her deepest thoughts turned inward once again.

When you love a man, its like sailing off the end of the world. You have no idea where you'll hit land. It was that kind of love that brought her into this insane mess. She stretched her legs, getting as comfortable as she could in the cramped space, with the seatbelt tight around her abdomen. The same kind of love her dad has for her mother. They hold nothing back. Storybook kind of love. And yours? What kind of love is yours, Leatha's words rang in her head-- fun time for Al, with little risk. Hell no. Well then, what? She shut off the internal voice, for now. The plane was about to touch ground.

Scooter was at the gate to meet them. Heleena held Karen back, signaling her to let the other passengers leave first. When they walked out, without a word to anyone, he took Judy into his arms. She hugged him too, and then dropped her arms. For the first time since they left Dover, there was the faintest smile on her face. That big plait had come undone again and her hair was swinging wild. Her father thought she had the most beautiful hair in the world. Of course, every time he told her that, Karen would comment that he came from a family of picky-headed women, so any kind of hair would be exciting to him.

"Could it be you are jealous?" He'd teased her more than once.

"Come on. I want to go home. We need to bathe, and clean any trace of that filthy place from our bodies." Karen started to walk pass him, but her husband was still looking over his baby.

"You're okay, honey?"

She just hunched her shoulders, head slightly bent.

"Please come on." Karen's patience was wearing thin.

"Karen, give him a break. He wants to be sure she's okay. We're home now. You can relax. Everything will be all right."

* * *

Fourteen calls in one day, but she didn't bother to keep track. Voices pushed her to keep calling. Each time one of the house members answered the phone, Arieta was called to respond to her questions.

"Have you heard from him? Where is he?"

The answer never varied. They had not received a single call from Peter.

She'd been home three days. Her thoughts returned to the last weeks -- new happiness with new friends. Even though Judy had been out of the house only twice since the day they brought her home, throughout each day she sat in her room by the phone.

Karen, however, was secretly grateful he'd made no attempt to contact her. She and Scooter believed Judy could get on with her life. They'd arranged for her to begin therapy next week. Everyone agreed that was what she needed.

As the week wore on, however, she showed no signs her emotional state was improving. She stayed in her room, refusing food and would not even agree to let Aunt Heleena come up to visit her the first day she tried.

Heleena persisted and returned the next evening. This time Judy opened the door.

She held her head down, not really looking at Heleena. Her eyes focused somewhere just below Heleena's elbow, looking at something only she could see. Heleena drew her over to the chair in front of her mirror. She found the brush and began brushing her hair and talking in a low soothing voice.

"Have you talked to Peter?" She knew the answer was no, but felt Judy needed to talk about him again.

"No. I don't know where he is."

"Have you called his place in Baltimore?"

"I went over there twice, but it was empty."

She stilled Heleena's hand and turned to face her, this time looking directly into her eyes. All of a sudden she sparked with life, eyes glittering.

"I can't live without him Aunt Heleena. I just can't. He's all I have." She said it with so much feeling, Heleena forgot, for a moment, the trauma she'd just experienced. There were no words of comfort she could give. So she hugged her tightly.

Karen, too, had remained around the house, just in case she was able to break through her daughter's hopeless mien. By Friday night she was climbing the walls. Frustrated and not getting anywhere with Judy, she and Scooter decided to go out for the evening. She'd been so withdrawn they didn't bother to invite her.

Before they left, Karen called through her bedroom door, letting her know they were leaving, but she didn't answer. Her attempt to open the door failed as it was locked.

They'd asked Heleena to join them, but she declined.

* * *

It felt like a womb -- dark, cozy and comforting. The only light being the red numbers of the digital clock shining on the dashboard.

The two-year-old import showed only seventeen thousand miles and most of them were put on the car in the last nine months. It was due for a tune-up.

There were no tears. Perhaps if she'd cried, events may have taken a different turn.

She could not recall just when she knew he was gone from her. Fear of his leaving her behind must have been like a seed ready to germinate. When the conditions were ready it bloomed.

"Peter, Peter. I love you. I'm so sleepy."

She saw a ten-year old with two long braids. The girl looked like her but her hair was fried. She looked scared --Now there were three girls in swimsuits - brown girls -- all ten -- maybe twelve, she was unable to tell. One of them looked like her too.

"I don't like it here mommie."

That same girl who looked like her was now sixteen. She still looked scared in this beautiful school.

Finally falling asleep, the little girl wasn't ready to go. She ran after Junior -- caught up with him and held his hand, tightly. His face was angry.

The girl tried to explain. She looked up at him. "I did everything she told me to do."

He didn't care. She pleaded with him. Suddenly, he stopped and looked into her eyes. The beautiful loving face was the same, but the mouth was different. They were not the lips that kissed hers so lovingly, this man's mouth was hard, unsmiling and mocking.

There was one tear left. It rolled down her cheek -- crystal clear. She drifted off -- the images constantly changing.

* * *

The shrill sound of the phone caused her to jump. She reached for the receiver, but had to leave the bed to get it, draping the sheet around her waist. Telephone calls in the middle of the night did not bring good news.

"Hello."

There were only screams coming from the other end of the receiver. For a minute she was numb.

She didn't recognize the voice at first, even though the woman kept calling her name.

"Who is this?"

"It's me Heleena, it's me, oh God."

Fully awake now, "Karen, what is it, what's wrong?"

"My baby, my baby, come quick, please, please." Then a piercing scream.

Al left the bed and came around to stand behind her, pulling her to his chest. "Who is it?"

"It's Karen, something's wrong, but she won't say what it is."

Scooter was on the phone now, "Heleena something terrible has happened."

"What?"

"Heleena, Judy is dead. She killed herself."

For the first time in her life, Heleena fainted.

It caught Al by surprise as the phone slipped from her hand. As he laid her on the bed he could hear the hysterical voice coming from the receiver on the floor.

He quickly revived Heleena and retrieved the phone from the floor. When she sat up, her back against his chest, he handed her the phone.

"Scooter what happened? When?"

The tremors running through her body caused her hand holding the receiver to shake. Al snatched the phone from her.

"Scooter, what the hell's going on?"

"Its Judy. She's dead."

"What?"

"She's dead, Al she...."

"Dead, how?"

"She killed herself Al. She killed herself," he said sobbing.

"We'll be right there."

"Get dressed, we need to get over there quickly."

The shock of the news temporarily paralyzed her, but she hurriedly dressed. Al was ready to leave within minutes. She grabbed her purse and slipped on soft flats.

Barely twenty minutes had passed from the time the phone rang when the Targa roared out of the driveway.

It was only then that either spoke.

"Poor, poor Judy. What made her do it?"

"I don't know, I didn't ask, I just thought we ought to get there in a hurry."

"Did he say how?"

"No."

Rosalind W. Johnson

Chapter 12

"I am the resurrection, and the life: he that believeth in me, though he were dead, yet shall he live: And whosoever liveth and believeth in me shall never die, Believest thou this?"

The minister's deep voice intoning the ageless and powerful scripture from the Gospel of St. John resonated through every corner of the magnificent edifice. Reverend Burns walking behind the casket, being rolled forward by two young men, was followed by Junior, then Karen and Scooter flanked by Heleena and Al.

Mt. Olive is a large church, but today every pew would be occupied. Heleena saw that the church was almost filled to capacity and there were many more people waiting outside.

Karen had not wanted a night funeral. Heleena was relieved when they decided on a daylight service. Saturday was the day of choice because almost anyone who wanted to come would be able to attend. They'd also decided to have an hour for people to greet the family just prior to the formal service. I never thought Karen would want this type of service, an old fashion funeral. Although Heleena surveyed the scene around her, she was very much aware of Karen at her side. The sedatives she'd taken earlier had calmed her, but her emotional hold on events was tenuous.

The family procession continued solemnly down the long aisle until they reached the front pews. Two men maneuvered the casket into place, and then stopped behind Reverend Burns. The beautiful family spray made entirely of Birds of Paradise was just removed and each young man took his place on each side of the casket, waiting. With the lift of his hand Reverend Burns signaled to them to open the casket. As he stood aside a hush descended over the gathering.

Heleena put her arm through Karen's and grasped her hand, interlocking their fingers. She took a deep breath and whispered close to Karen's ear "Take all the time you need."

"Oh Heleena she looks just like she's sleeping." Tears streamed down her face.

Tugging her hand from Heleena's, she reached out and touched her daughter's cold cheek. Those in line behind her waited patiently. "My baby, oh my baby," Scooter moaned.

Heleena blinked back tears, knowing she needed to be strong for them.

"My poor, poor little baby girl," He was crying openly now. Soon she'd be no more, only a memory.

Junior, too, dry-eyed, reached out and touched his sister, but kept his mourning locked away somewhere inside him, out of sight. He would let go of her a little at a time, as he was able to handle the loss.

Finally, Heleena studied the face in repose. Judy had been a lovely child, the perfect combination of her parents. The beautiful head of hair she'd inherited from some family member back up the line, now lay forever spread around her face. The photogenic wide set eyes were her daddy's and that caramel color, a true blend of both parents. She'd been tall and graceful. Now she lay sleeping the final sleep, but still a beauty. The soft pink gown was a compliment to her color even in death.

Heleena gently took Karen's arm and guided her to the place reserved for them. Junior and Scooter immediately followed.

The crowd began the slow process of viewing the body and greeting the family. All these people will never pass through here in one hour. Every person will want to gaze on the body of this young angel, some just for curiosity's sake. Heleena carried on an internal conversation while shaking hands of the mourners. She kept a smile on her face making comments of appreciation. Many of the people she knew, but there was a sizable number she'd never seen before or didn't remember. She was satisfied, however, that Karen would be pleased at the great outpouring of sympathy.

Forty-five minutes after they'd entered the church Heleena turned around to see how the crowd was progressing. The line still stretched out of the door. Even some of the people who had been sitting in the church when they arrived were now joining the slow moving line. When the mourners came by to shake the hands of Karen and Scooter or to press a kiss, she and Al were treated in the same manner, as family.

As the crowd passed, Heleena was sure there were those who thought the seating arrangements strange. She sat next to Karen and Al was next to Scooter. No one could deny them this right. They'd been outside the delivery room when she entered the world and they intended to be just as close to her parents in seeing her to her final resting place. Marva sat to Heleena's left followed by Karen's mom, her two sisters, their husbands, and her aunts. Heleena's children, Selena, and Judy's young cousin sat behind them. Scooter's family, though smaller than Karen's were all there. They sat on the first two rows across the aisle. On the row with them were Greg and two of Judy's childhood friends.

Heleena noticed Karen was holding up surprisingly well. She couldn't tell about Scooter, but was sure Al remained aware of his emotional state. If necessary they would stop the line and begin formal services. They'd been up since five and Karen had not gone to sleep until three, only after Al gave her a sedative.

She'd insisted on going to the funeral parlor again this morning. When they called the undertaker, he immediately sent a car for them. Karen's mother and Scooter's sister went with them. They were out of the house and back before the others began to stir.

Mrs. Anderson was so overwhelmed with grief, Heleena had to hire someone else to see to household matters until she was able to assume her duties. There were fifteen people staying in the house, including Heleena, who had not been home but once since Karen's terrifying call last Friday night. Just recalling her screams made

Heleena shiver. Karen reached over and lightly rubbed the back of her hand.

The air inside the church was becoming stuffy, even with the state-of-the-art air conditioning system. Reverend Burns was standing calmly to the right of the casket appearing unruffled, wrapped in solemn dignity. Karen and Scooter had contributed big sums of money to the building fund. In the last ten years the size of the church had doubled and the Reverend stood proudly.

At last the line started to thin. Soft and low, the choir, began singing –

> *Swing low sweet chariot*
> *Coming for to carry me home*
> *Swing low, sweet chariot*
> *Coming for to carry me home*

Collectively, the entire congregation sat back to absorb the sweet music, waiting for the minister to give some explanation for the untimely demise of such a beautiful young creature.

> *I looked over Jordan and what did I see*
> *Coming for to carry me home*
> *I looked over Jordan and what did I see*
> *Coming for to carry me home.*

Those who were sitting close enough to see them cast their eyes at the family to see how they were taking it -- how they were holding up under the pressure.

> *A band of angels coming after me*
> *Coming for to carry me home*
> *A band of angels coming after me*
> *Coming for to carry me home.*

Reverend Burns' booming voice spread throughout the edifice "Yes, a band of Angels coming after me. Swing low, sweet chariot. And He said, I am the resurrection and the life, and whosoever believeth on me shall never die, yes, shall never die"

Heleena drifted away, still observing, still alert, but calling forth in her mind images across these years of friendship, trying to pinpoint the one image to explain the reason they sat mourning the end of a life that should just be beginning.

"She is not gone. She is just away -- And yet she lives, but in a far, far better place," the Reverend intoned.

Karen's mother, Ms. DeBeau, had begun to perspire profusely. She was moaning and rocking from side to side, her sweating arms rubbing against Marva. Heleena never cared for Mrs. DeBeau. The first thing out of her mouth was always to tell Judy to stay out of the sun, so she wouldn't get so dark. Now here she is, carrying on as if she'd been a loving and supportive grandmother.

Reverend Burns continued, "When we search our hearts, minds, even the scriptures, we come away, still asking why? Why, oh Father, why? In the flower of her time the Almighty called her home, to sit on the throne of Glory." His words rumbled through the church. "But, for those who loved her, for all who knew her, the earthly question remains, why?"

The congregation sat mesmerized. Reverend Burns, known for his outstanding oratory did not fail to deliver today.

Karen's sobs wracked her body. To hear her crying like that broke Heleena's heart. Scooter reached across Junior and held her hand tightly. Even as he grieved openly, he sought to comfort her. To hold back her own tears, Heleena examined the many flower arrangements, one by one - carnations so red they seemed to be colored by blood -- Blue Deliahs, Lilies whose texture was like the virgin skin of a young girl. The beautiful Tiger Lilies seemed so out of place here. They were of the type to grace an elegant room or hallway, rather than to stand as a symbol of death. She wiped a tear.

Once again her mind drifted back over the initial family events of this last week. Karen was so hysterical when they arrived at the house, they summoned her doctor. Whatever he gave her put her to sleep immediately. Scooter in a daze, could do nothing. She'd called their families. Surprisingly, they came immediately. In the mist of her thoughts, she was startled when Reverend Burns began his final pronouncement.

"When that great day comes and we're all together again, there will be no tears, no crying--only joy, love, and fellowship at the throne of Him who made us all. So, as we bid a brief farewell to this beautiful and fragile one who slipped away to await the Grand Reunion--Praise be to God Almighty."

When he took his seat, on the raised platform behind the pulpit, the audience seemed to pause, catching its collective breath. Heleena turned, the sea of faces waited expectantly.

The choir began to sing "Take My Hand Precious Lord." They began low, then steady voices building right along with the congregation's outpouring of grief. Heleena had held herself together for Karen's sake, but now she broke down, her tears flowing freely, slipping down her face. She nervously twisted the soft linen handkerchief held tightly in her hand. When the soloist began another verse, she shuddered.

Once the music reached a crescendo every person in the church felt the loss. As Reverend Burns descended the pulpit two ladies in white uniforms moved from their places along the wall to stand near the family. The two young men who stood on either side of the casket throughout the service now gently rolled it first to the right for a final viewing by Scooter's small family, then toward Karen and Scooter. They lowered it for Karen and Scooter to take one last look at the cherished face. Heleena was hypnotized. The casket seemed to be moving in slow motion, coming towards them while appearing to stand still.

At Karen's scream, she jumped. Karen was reaching for the box, Scooter tried to restrain her, switching seats with his son. The two ladies stood waiting. When the casket was stopped directly in front of them Karen leaned over, her head resting on the side of the box. The mournful sobs coming from her were dreadful--sounds a mother should never have to make.

Finally, Scooter was able to pull her back from touching the beloved face; he folded her into his arms, calming her while his own tears flowed unchecked. The young men slowly rolled the casket to the end of the pew in front of Karen's relatives. The people in the pew behind them craned forward to look on the face of their loved one again, to imprint in their minds forever, the once loving familiar face. The casket was then rolled back to its original place, the top carefully closed.

What Heleena had feared all along finally happened. Karen fainted. Had Scooter not had his arms around her she would have fallen to the floor. Her head dropped, hanging over his arm. The two ladies in white rushed forward, one assisting Scooter and Al in holding her, the other breaking a small vial of smelling salts. Al snatched it from her pushing it under Karen's nose. Shortly, she began thrashing her head back and forth, arms flailing. People in the rear were straining to see the commotion up front.

When she was calm, Scooter held her face against his shoulder so she could not immediately see that the casket had been rolled away down the aisle. It was now being loaded into the hearse. Not a soul moved to leave the church. They were all waiting for the family to precede them.

Karen had to be helped by her husband and son as she moved slowly down the aisle toward the door, Heleena and Al directly behind them.

No one in the car spoke during the ride to the cemetery. Each lost in private thoughts. The undertaker had police escorts. More than forty cars followed the hearse. Karen never left the limousine and Heleena remained inside with her. The driver pulled along side the open grave. He'd parked so they looked directly on the graveside proceedings. They held hands throughout the short ceremony. Every car was out of site before the gleaming bronze coffin was lowered into the vault and covered with dirt.

Back at the house Karen and Scooter immediately secluded themselves in the master bedroom wing on the second floor. Heleena also went up to change and was back downstairs in ten minutes, to oversee the receiving of guests and food distribution. Although they'd hired help, she needed to make sure everything moved smoothly.

Karen's mom had plopped down in the high backed wing chair near the fireplace in the living room -- better to survey the crowd in her usual critical manner. The house was filling with people fast.

Heleena and Anne were moving among the guests, helping with whatever was needed.

"Ms. DeBeau, can I get you anything?" Heleena asked.

"Yes honey. I saw some pies back there, bring me two small pieces, and two or three pieces of the fried chicken and a little potato salad."

"Something to drink?"

"Glass of ice tea."

Before her three daughters decided to request personal service, Heleena beckoned them to come with her. "Cecilia, why don't you, Lelie, and Marie come and get something, before the best is picked over or we run out of what you may want."

There was no way they'd run out of food. Visitors continuously streamed in with plates and platters piled high with chicken, cooked every way imaginable, but mostly fried and everything else to go with it.

Ms. Anderson, who had worked for Karen since Scooter's first paycheck as a young intern, was supervising everything in the kitchen. "How's Mrs. Topley doing?" She asked Heleena.

"Still not talking. She hasn't said anything since we left the cemetery."

"What about the Doctor?"

"It's hard to say."

"She loved that child better than herself. She just wanted everything in life to be perfect for her. Sometimes I think she loved too much. She wanted no mistakes for the baby."

Heleena thoughtfully did not interrupt her, knowing Mrs. Anderson was also experiencing the terrible grief.

"Sometimes you just have to let your children stumble and stump their toes, then they'll began to watch where they're walking. Parents have to let them make their mistakes, so they can learn from them. You know what I mean?"

"Yes, but its hard to let them make mistakes, when you know the possible consequences."

"That's true. But how can they learn to decide for themselves if we jump in to push aside every little thing we think is a nuisance?"

Mrs. Anderson kept talking, not waiting for or expecting an answer.

"That child never even had a chance to pick out her own clothes. And that beautiful head of hair--never could wear it the way she liked." She stopped arranging food on trays to wipe her eyes.

"Why don't you go to your old room for a while."

"No, no, I'm okay. Just thinking about my poor baby, gone like that, causes me so much anger--not at Mrs. Topley or her dad, but just how life treats people. She was such a cute little thing. I remember the first day she went to school. She wore a yellow pinafore. Two huge yellow bows on each side of her head, all that hair hanging down her back."

"She did have the most beautiful hair I've ever seen on a child. That dark deep, deep brown which took on a sparkling color during the summer months when she was out in the sun so much."

"The only time I ever heard the doctor chastise Ms. Topley, it was about that child's hair. When she started junior high school, Mrs. Topley had it straightened with chemicals. When he came home and saw it he started to sweat, right here in the kitchen. He hollered at Mrs. Topley, told her if she ever did it again she'd pay a terrible price. He was so mad, he stormed out of the house. Through it all little Judy was standing there looking like a wet kitten, that beautiful hair plastered to her head."

Both of them were thinking of the youngster, now gone from them.

"I think I'll run upstairs and look in on her," Mrs. Anderson said.

"If you need me, call on the intercom."

She went through the pantry and up the back stairs. Heleena stood alone in the kitchen until a group of guests joined her. They were people she knew. Her eyes opened wider when she saw two impressive looking men follow the group into the kitchen.

"Stanley," she called. "I'm so glad you could come." Hugging him closely, she kissed him on the cheek. "Where did you find him?" she asked, turning to Floyd.

"I got in touch with him right after I heard, but he was in a big trial and could only now get away."

"When I arrived at the church, all of you were seated, so I took a seat in the back," Stanley told her.

"How is Big Time holding up?" He asked, referring to the nickname he first put on Karen because of her often stated desires to be big time, when they were in law school.

"As you can guess, this is a terrible, terrible time for her. But she'll want to see you before you leave."

"Oh, I'm not leaving until I have a chance to talk to both of them."

Heleena took each one by the hand and led them to the small curved glass-enclosed room off the kitchen. The two men sat in low chairs opposite each other and Heleena sat on a hassock between them.

They were still two fine looking men. Both starting to gray, with a little less hair than they had when they were in law school, but still able to turn any woman's head. Stanley was a U.S. Court of Appeals Judge and Floyd was a U.S. District Court Judge in DC. Floyd had been Law Journal Editor and she'd heard his decisions reflected that background.

"What happened?"

"In these last years she was very unhappy, unsure of herself. Then she became involved with someone who took advantage of her, her naiveté. You know how it is -- there are so many of our youngsters searching for something -- something they feel they need."

"She was such a darling girl. I last saw her four years ago, just before Bea passed. We were up here at NIH for some experimental treatment as a last ditch effort to cure her. Since the treatment took all day, I called them and came by. Judy was home, pretty as a picture."

"Has it really been four years since Bea passed?"

"Yes, four years this past spring."

"Unh Unh, it seems like yesterday."

"At our age time moves at a fast clip."

"Too fast."

"Every time I see you though, time seems to stand still," Stanley told her, teasingly.

"You're still number one," Floyd added.

"You two have always been on my case from the very first day we met. What I'd like to know though is what's with you two now that both of you are single?"

Stanley couldn't hide the surprise look on his face. "You asking for yourself?"

"No, not the way you think. I'm simply curious to know what's with two good-looking highly eligible guys? Floyd, I'm really surprised you're still walking around free. What's wrong with these women?"

"I'm not interested in taking the plunge again." He held his hands, palms up, in a gesture of surrender. "Forget it. All the trouble I had getting out of that trap. I'd rather jump from a bridge, than walk down the aisle again."

"Excuse me," she laughed. Floyd had a rocky marriage, to put it mildly. Riva was a mean and jealous big red woman. She thought any woman who talked to Floyd was sleeping with him. He claimed he would have left her years before he did, but could not afford to leave. The same summer his last child graduated, he moved out, giving Riva sole ownership of their home and moved into an apartment. They had no other assets. Floyd had struggled for years in a small practice and with the repeat business and referrals from his earliest clients and their families and friends he made a good living and a solid income flow. Then he went on the bench. His three girls were able to attend private schools right on through college. Since the divorce he'd brought a nice townhouse in northwest Washington and appeared to be enjoying his freedom. His emphatic statement of not wanting to marry again was clearly understandable.

As they talked quietly, people came and went in a steady stream.

"Excuse me guys, I need to check on Karen and Scooter." She stood and turned to leave when Stanley reminded her to give Karen his love.

Upstairs she stopped by her room first just to center herself. She was feeling the strain, but still determined not to give in to her own grief, not yet anyway. When she knocked on their door, there was a feeble "come in." Scooter was the only one in the sitting room. He sat on the sofa in his shirt sleeves, without a tie, staring at nothing.

"Have you had anything to eat?"

"A little something. Mrs. Anderson brought up a couple of plates."

When she looked at the table behind the sofa, nothing had been eaten. She checked on Karen, who was lying across the bed, asleep.

After straightening the bed covers, she quietly closed the door and went back downstairs to circulate among the guests.

She sent her children home after the crowd thinned to about ten people. Scooter had come down once, but Karen remained upstairs all afternoon. Junior wandered about trying to be brave, but he could not mask the sadness that sat like a heavy weight in his eyes. Everyone offered comforting words which he accepted with quiet grace so like his father.

After sitting on their wide butts eating all afternoon, Ms. DeBeau and Karen's sisters finally returned to their bedrooms. The sisters' husbands remained downstairs with Al, Marva, and a handful of other close friends.

The girls they hired to pick up and clean after the guests, did a marvelous job. The guests ate most of the food and leftovers were put away for the family's consumption tomorrow. Later, the closest friends gathered together in the family room. The tension in all of them, obvious.

"An old fashion funeral. It surprised me," Billie said.

"It was Karen's idea. All the songs were picked by her," Heleena replied. "We tried to get her to let us handle some of the more mundane details, but she refused."

"It's understandable." Al said, wearily pressing his forehead. He'd loosened his tie and removed his jacket. He too, had been with Scooter almost continuously since they'd received the sad news. Someone else was looking after his patients.

"Al you know Scooter better than anyone else, he seems so calm, is he suppressing his grief?"

"I think he's more concerned about Karen now, and Junior. I'll go up and check on him again before we leave tonight. He needs sleep. He's been up the last two nights and refuses to take anything to help him sleep."

"Each of them will have to grieve in the only way they know how," Marva said. "Their loss will be a long time healing. We just have to be here for them. They need us more than ever now. Poor Karen, this was something she could never, ever have seen coming, not in a million years."

Heleena could not stop yawning. She was sitting at the end of the sofa with her feet tucked under a cushion and her head resting on the arm. She didn't realize she was napping until she heard Karen's hesitant, "Hi everybody."

They stared at her, everyone momentarily speechless. Then they began to speak at once. Her appearance downstairs was unexpected.

"Come over here and sit down sweetheart." Al got up and gently guided her to the sofa.

Heleena moved closer encircling Karen in her arms. Marva too, took her place next to Karen. She and Heleena were looking her over and neither liked what they saw. Her color, what little she had, was completely washed away. She looked gray and her eyes were ringed with dark circles. The blouse and pants she wore hung loosely. She seemed to be skin and bones. Even her hair looked lifeless.

"I'll get you a small plate of food, you need to eat something," Heleena told her as she rose from the sofa.

"No, don't. I can't eat anything."

"You need food in your stomach. I'll open a can of soup then. Anybody want coffee?" Only two people said yes.

Two hours later Heleena was having difficulty falling asleep. She and Karen had remained in the family room after the others went home, just talking mostly about events of the past week. Karen confided in her that just prior to Judy leaving for Florida she had thought Peter might have been involved in something illegal.

"When I discussed my suspicion with Scooter he thought my imagination was over-reaching because of my intense dislike for Peter.

After we found her, all he could say was, "You were right."

Rosalind W. Johnson

Chapter 13

A week had passed since the funeral. To their credit Karen's family stayed on until yesterday. Scooter's people left the day after the funeral. There'd never been any love lost between the two families.

However, everyone was reluctant to part. Judy's death so quick, was a tragedy without history for all of them. They needed to turn it over in their minds, reflect on the event, and look in their corners to see if the villain lived near them.

Three old friends, still tight, once again, sharing life's vicissitudes. Daylight was reluctant to quit, so they sat in semi-darkness, nursing their drinks; each man, for a moment, secluded in his own thoughts.

Al never realized until this tragedy how much he, too, needed the comfort of his buddies. He'd suggested they bring Scooter to his office so they could soothe their individual pains and give him a few hours out of the storm.

The frenzied days leading to her funeral and burial had taken a terrible toll on them. And the grieving had not really begun in earnest. They'd surrounded Scooter and Karen so their lost was held at bay, for a time anyway. His home right now was no place for him to replay the life of his baby, to cry for her, wallow in his sorrow if he chose, and gradually begin to say goodbye.

They huddled like warriors of old, safe in the cave, away from their women, finally being human and sharing secrets.

"Remember, Dr. Mims?" Scooter was first to break the silence.

"Who could forget him? The worst Don Juan for miles around," Greg said.

"No question. But, there was a lot of truth in what he told us."

"What brought him to mind?"

"He was by the house Wednesday night. My mother-in-law was taken with him."

"I'm not surprised. He chased every skirt he could find when we were in school."

"But I liked him. He was fair and wasn't always beating up on the students."

"All we had to do was make sure none of us moved in on his territory." Greg was not that interested in Dr. Mims, but it meant something to Scooter that he came to sit with the family.

"It was thoughtful of him to come and express his sympathy in person. Karen never liked him, so she was suspicious of his reasons for being there."

Greg couldn't contain himself, "Man, Karen would never have been your wife, if you'd listened to him."

"We thought we were invincible. He'd been down the same road and knew we were vulnerable. He was always good with the students. He even came to the cabaret."

"I wanted to come, but my schedule wouldn't cooperate."

Al stretched his legs settling more comfortably in his chair. "You missed a good time. At least forty-five people came back. With the invited guests there were between 175 and 200 people."

"How much scholarship money did we raise?"

"With all the pledges the total came to $233,000."

"I'll be damned."

Al and Greg were carrying the conversation, but both of them constantly kept a protective eye on Scooter, who silently sipped his drink. There was little more they could say to him that would ease his grief, so the comfort of their presence would have to be enough.

With them he could sit and look inward, remembering his child, and not, as in the past few days, constantly respond to expressions of sympathy. With these two friends there was no pressure to join in small talk. He felt a release, finally, after being numb for days. All his efforts had been toward Karen, helping her get through each day. For a few precious hours he could now lean into his own turbulent feelings.

"It's hard for me to believe we've been out of school twenty five years."

"The time slips away, faster every year.

"I'll tell you this, I'm starting to look forward to retirement."

"Do you think you'll stay in Atlanta?"

"Probably not. Lisa would like to move to the Islands. We invested in a piece of property down there last year, not too far from the water."

"Sounds like you'll be pulling in the shingle soon."

"If you recall, we were barely out of school when we all talked about retiring in the islands."

"We made all kinds of plans during the euphoria of the times, with the world in front of us."

"And then there were the plans that were made for us."

They looked at him and both of them knew his thoughts. Scooter was a doctor's doctor, but his entire working life was solely to power the engine of Karen's plans and schemes. To tell the truth, no one could honestly say, what plans Scooter had for himself when he graduated.

"Most of the guys have retirement on their minds. All of them sick of the endless forms and authorizations which are necessary now. Just about anybody who has practiced at least twenty years is overwhelmed with paper. If you don't have at least two or three people handling the paperwork you're out of business. The first year I was in practice one person did all the paperwork. Now, we have a small staff that does nothing but process forms."

"Exactly. That's just why I'm looking forward to getting out."

Al's appraisal of Greg was unsettling. He was alert to any reference to Heleena. Since he'd been in town he and Heleena had been together more than once and the atmosphere was friendly camaraderie, nothing more. But they'd had an easy divorce -- he wanted out and she didn't protest.

The children wanted him to stay at home while he was here, but he opted to stay with Al and Marva. Not really knowing his Washington friends, Lisa didn't come up for the funeral, leaving Greg to share the communal grief without her.

"Scooter, you and Karen need to get away for awhile. Why don't you come down to Atlanta and visit us for a couple of weeks?"

"I don't think so, not now. I couldn't get Karen to leave home anytime soon."

"I understand, but if you change your mind, the invitation stands."

"I know Heleena and Marva are planning to take her to St. Maartin soon."

"They're still like three peas in a pod, huh?"

"Just the same, as close as the day they met. Not one day goes by that Karen is not on the phone with Heleena or Marva and sometimes the three of them are on the phone together."

"It's amazing how close they are and how different they are. Even after Heleena and I were married, I thought they were the same person with three different faces."

"Greg, I've said it to you many times, you never really knew Heleena."

"I came to understand that. I knew from the beginning there was a certain aloofness about her, but I thought she would lose some of it when we married. But I can say this for her, she looks damn good. I can't put my finger on it, but she looks younger, more alive, or something. The way a woman looks when she's involved, you know in love, having an affair."

"As far as I know, she's not involved with anyone, if she were, Karen would have said something."

"Even the children noticed the change in her."

Al's eyes were steady and his voice never wavered "One thing's for sure she is the kind of woman any man would want. You're not having second thought's are you?"

"No. Our marriage was like a thousand others during that time, something expected, but destined for failure, at some point."

"Why do you say that?"

"We didn't fit."

"Al and I were both surprised she married you. You were a little flashy for her."

"Like I said it was that particular time. Everybody else was getting married. I was smitten by her, as they say. So, we did the do." He hunched his shoulders in a gesture of resignation.

Al fought back the resentment that wouldn't stay put. He couldn't help feeling Greg had stolen a part of his dream. Even now, the smell of her was in his nostrils. He rose, refilled his glass and changed the course of his thoughts.

"If we could relive our young lives, we'd delete certain decisions we made when we thought we had every angle figured."

"Funny how you think about life when you're young. Only one opinion is important and that's your own. Then a lifetime later, you're not so sure any more. Wrong turns on one-way streets."

"You started over, in the marriage department, at least."

"Nothing's different though. When women become wives, they don't work as hard."

"My wife has not changed since our first date."

They laughed. For sure Karen had not changed. She began spending Scooter's money before they even tied the knot.

"You'd probably welcome a little change, wouldn't you man?" This wasn't the first time Greg had teased him about Karen.

"But, getting back to my ex-wife -- something has to be happening in her life. She was more pleasant to me than the last time we met. Al, you ought to know. She was always close to you."

"She's herself. She is going in other directions now. With you, she was more a wife and mother. Outside of her work, she gave herself to you guys. Lately, the very personal woman has emerged. She's certainly no longer a wife, but she needs to be more than a mother and a lawyer."

"Do you think she has her eyes on somebody?"

"Heh man, why should that matter to you?" Scooter sensed there was more behind Greg's question than the casual interest of an ex-husband who walked away for what appeared to be no good reason.

"I don't know, but she's lit up, shining, ripe."

"And damn sure your loss." There was a cutting edge to Al's voice. "And you can't go back."

"There's no such thing as can't."

"Believe me, you cannot yoke her a second time."

I wonder if our friendship could have lasted, had he and Heleena settled someplace else. I really thought he knew I intended to have her for my date that first night. But he jumped right in and grabbed her for himself. To this day it is still unclear whether he really knew her or cared.

The only reason I consented to that date was the expectation that she'd be with me. But, in the blink of an eye she was snatched away, by a man who didn't even know the type of woman she is.

"The two of you always took her side in every situation."

"Your side was always just too complicated."

The room was thick with remembering. Even grief sat quietly in the corner for a time. The three of them needed to connect loose threads, fill in the blanks and make things right.

Al's heart turned as he again remembered the anger he felt when Greg made his claim on Heleena. They'd been out together twice. Greg was planning their next date and confidently made the statement that she was in the bag. His frustration mounted.

Even during their brief break-up, before the marriage, he was in a position to cut off forever Greg's relationship with her. Her attraction to Greg was not as strong as he believed. Her ego was bruised, not much more. His advice to her had been to do nothing, if Greg were serious he'd contact her. He really didn't think Greg was serious, but within weeks he'd repaired their break.

"Once again, you are showing your insensitivity where Heleena is concerned. This time, though, the laugh is on you."

"Probably.

"Are you thinking about joining one of these new health alliances?" He asked, switching the direction of the conversation.

"I don't have any choice man."

"Any physician who thinks he can practice in his own isolated world, will soon be out of business. You lose your patients to some other group. It's simple, you join or you die."

"You joining too?" He asked Scooter.

"Yes. I'm going in with Al's group."

Al grabbed the phone in the middle of the first ring. It was Heleena.

"How's Scooter holding up?"

"We're fine, probably need to send out for some food."

"Just checking. Karen wanted to know how he's faring."

"That was Heleena," he said replacing the receiver.

"She's still checking everything with you. That use to bug the hell out of me and she never even realized how I felt."

The burning sensation in the pit of his stomach just wouldn't quit. Al was grateful for the murky shadows cast by low light in the room. His eyes blazed in the darkness.

"She was always saying, Al said this or Al said that."

"But it was to you that she said I do and I bet she'd laugh if she could hear you now."

"I wouldn't bet too much."

You sure wouldn't find it funny if you knew how she viewed her marriage to you, he thought. "Let's get something to eat. What do you want?" Al looked at his watch "It's almost twelve. We might be able to get pizza. I'm sure nothing else is available at this late hour."

Even though he found Greg's comments disconcerting, he had a nagging need to hear more of his friend's reflections, just to fill in the missing pieces.

"Since my baby left here I've been thinking constantly about her life, my life and whether I would do many things differently," Scooter said.

"I can't tell you the times I've gone through that drill myself, and it's a mother too."

Scooter obviously had something on his mind. They were mellow now. They'd almost consumed a fifth of Scotch. The shadows in the room danced just enough to provide protection as they revealed secrets hidden from each other for so long.

"Tell us." Al coaxed him.

Scooter dived right in. "My wife--I think I would have tried to know her better."

"Having second thoughts," Greg teased him.

"Not in the way you're thinking. I was attracted by my perception of her. To me she was like someone from another world, and she sought me out. I was flattered, she made me feel, for once, that I could have the prize. It was a heady experience and she was so beautiful. When we first started dating I would prepare every time for that date to be our last. I just couldn't believe I had any kind of future with her."

He lapsed into silence, his mind reaching back, trying to recapture a younger Scooter, shy, little experience with women, awed by this beautiful creature with soft hair. "She was quick and soothing, like warm cocoa. The first time I saw her, she waltzed up to me in the library and boldly introduced herself."

"I've been watching you for several nights. Don't you ever take a break from these books?" she asked pointing to the thick books, opened in front of him.

She'd responded to his puzzled and surprised look by touching the tip of his nose. It was electrifying, and she'd seen the effect on him.

"I won't bite, just thought I'd come over and introduce myself. I'm Karen DeBeau."

He was speechless. This was a first for him. He tried to smile, but the lopsided grin, she'd told him later, looked more like a grimace.

"And what's your name?" she asked, now reaching for his hand. Scooter stood up quickly extending his hand.

"William Topley. Have a seat." Without hesitation she sat beside him, still smiling. In that moment he'd opened himself to her and from that night on his happiness was to deny her nothing.

Scooter had no protection against Karen's onslaught. No frame of reference on how to relate to women, to know their cunning and enticing ways. There was no way for him to know then, that she'd been watching him for several days, for just the right time to spring her assault.

Scooter was just three months short of his twenty-fifth birthday. He was a serious person and a more serious student in his second year of medical school. The happy-go-lucky teenage years that most young men enjoyed had passed him by. He was not the type of boy pursued by girls. He'd never learn to laugh and flirt and live for the moment. Certainly his strong Negroid features did not draw the young girls of the mid '60's. So he found release in his studies, finishing first in his high school class.

Even in college he continued to excel, graduating with honors. Medical school was onerous, but not a problem for him. His steady plodding way saw him through his first year and into his second. While most students considered pharmacology and pathology the twin demons of the curriculum, they were no problem for him. He was studying for a pharmacology exam the night Karen stamped her brand on him. Thereafter, his life was never to be the same.

"Karen is not always what she appears to be. There are things in her life that scare her just as they do the rest of us."

"When you think back, none of us had long courtships," Al added. "You never get to really know a person until you live together."

"And then only under the banner of marriage," Greg said with a hard edge to his voice.

"What do you mean?"

"When two people live together, each one knows the way to the door out of the relationship. On the other hand, the legal entanglement of marriage grants an individual time to regroup, look at the other person and see if the relationship is worth salvaging."

"So, what are you saying," Al wanted to know.

"Well, just that no matter how long you're going with somebody, you just don't know the person. Take my wife for example, ex-wife, I mean. She was so enthusiastic when we were going together, how was I to know her coolness would assert itself after we were married."

Al was just a little afraid to wade into this even more, but he had to comment. The mixed feelings of resentment and curiosity, he was trying to stifle, came back in a rush. "It's hard to believe. All this talk about her being cool, you seem to be talking about another woman, somebody we don't know."

"You sure didn't know her as a wife. Our incompatibility stood between us from the beginning and only grew wider and wider, until we were so far apart we could not hide the gulf. There must have been a side of Marva you didn't see until you two tied the knot?"

"Oh yes. There were many things about her I didn't understand. Her mistrust for one."

"Would you marry her again?"

"What I wouldn't do is rush into a long term relationship. As a young man I should have explored my music more."

"Man, after we got out of Howard, we didn't have time for anything else."

"I mean even before med school. My music was important to me. I regret never taking time to see how far I could go, but mama convinced me to get another source of income, just in case."

"Well, we were sure the just-in-case-generation. Almost everything we did, we did just in case, that extra insurance. But, I never knew music was that important to you."

"That I squandered my chance to follow its lead is one of two mistakes I made in my youth."

"Who would have thought. You took to medicine with such gusto, it's hard to imagine you wanting to do anything different."

"Secret dream"

"You said there were two mistakes, fess up, what was the other?"

Al sipped his drink and stretched his legs. His relaxed position hid the internal turmoil. "Just another secret dream."

Tonight Greg wanted to talk. He'd missed Scooter and Al and maybe other aspects of his old life. Even being with them on this sad occasion couldn't mask his pleasure sitting around shooting the breeze with the guys who knew him, when.

By the time the pizza arrived, they were again lost in individual regrets and memories.

"Not a bad pizza for this time of night." Greg was eating with much gusto, which probably accounted for the extra inches around his waist.

"Since Richie came to live with us, pizza's in the house almost everyday. I think that is all the boy eats."

"Young people can live on the stuff, exclusively. Selena did the same thing when she had parties, pizza was the only food she served, with every topping imaginable."

"Kids live in a world of their own, don't they?"

"That is one true statement you can take to the bank." Al looked over at Scooter, but he didn't seem uncomfortable with the turn of the conversation.

"Heleena said he'd settled down since going to Atlanta."

"He has. Shortly after he arrived, he was ready to return here, but after a couple of months he adjusted. I was surprised Heleena didn't call more often to check on him."

"He needed to be away from here, he missed his brother and she'd started to spoil him."

"She did a wonderful job with the kids. I know it wasn't easy, but with me living in Atlanta, there was no way I could see them as much as I wanted to. But I think we're making up for the lost time."

"Whatever time you have with him is good time."

They held their breaths. Maybe Scooter was ready to talk about his loss, at last. Al was relieved.

"I should have spent more time with my baby. When she became withdrawn, I assumed she was just going through a temporary phase. Then she began seeing that bum. She was consumed by him. When the relationship first started, it was always, Peter this, Peter that, constantly."

"You know how young girls are. They wear their hearts for all the world to see."

"I think she was going through more than that. He became the dominant force in her life. She started staying out all night--over in Baltimore. She had to meet him. He rarely came to our house. He would call, and the next thing you know, she was out the door. Karen would rant and rage. But, it was no good. She only listened to him. I can't help but think there was more I could have done."

"Don't blame yourself. How one person feels about another, man or woman, is something no one else can figure. She was a woman with a woman's feelings. That is something you couldn't stop. Nobody could."

"She was still your little girl and her feelings for that SOB didn't diminish her love for you." Even in the dark, Al was able to see the anguish on his face. Suppose it was Selena lying in that cold grave. His heart nearly stopped. For a few seconds, he no longer heard his friend's agonizing voice. But in a moment he was wrenched back to the solemn room by grief stricken words which thundered in the darkness.

"She was pregnant. My poor baby was expecting a baby of her own." His tears began to flow.

Al and Greg were stunned. Silence descended like a bomb. The only sounds in the room were the sobs of a father whose heart was rendered.

Rosalind W. Johnson

Chapter 14

Twice in the last hour Heleena thought she heard the powerful hum of the Targa, however, each time she rushed to the side door, she was mistaken. She forced herself to relax by going to her youngest son's room and putting away the clothes he'd left thrown around the room. He was the only one of the three who depended on her help to keep him organized. Greg accused her of spoiling him. So what, he is my baby.

She sat on his bed thinking how much she'd enjoyed them, even during this sad time. Johnny was starting to look more like Greg. He still retained the I-know-what's-best attitude, but that was okay. At least it would keep him focused on his own plans. Anne had cut her hair to the quick, in the latest fashion. Her dad claimed it was just another flash of independence. He didn't care for the look at all, but would never give her the satisfaction of saying so. Anything they do without consulting him, signals defiance.

In a final act of desperation to calm herself, Heleena took a bath. She hadn't been alone with Al in two weeks. He'd called earlier today to say he would be at her house around seven. Something must have delayed him.

When the bell rang she calmly walked to the door, but when she saw his smiling lips, she rushed into his arms, breathing his scent. He held her close as she lifted her mouth to his.

His face was drawn. He looked tired, but of course none of them had slept much in the last two weeks.

"You haven't looked this dog eared since your residency days."

"That, sweetheart is putting it mildly. I feel like I've been through a tornado that lasted all day."

"Have you eaten dinner?"

"No. I'm not hungry, but I would like a drink. Make it scotch and water, please."

He sat on a stool at the end of the counter and watched her make the drink.

"So how are you holding up?"

"By my fingernails."

He reached for her and pulled her back into his arms, crossing his ankles behind her.

"Lately, life's been so unreal."

Arms around each other, they clung together. Heleena held his face in her hands, wanting so much to comfort him. "Why don't you have your drink and then really relax."

He responded by squeezing her tighter. He never did take more than two sips of the smooth mixture.

* * *

As they lay together, she could feel the tension in him. He was uncharacteristically quiet. Something was bothering him, but she was content to wait for him to say.

Just when she thought he must be asleep she felt the full force of his deep down sigh. She was anxious and wanted to know what was worrying him so, but hesitated to ask. Immediately, several of the possibilities she turned over in her mind alarmed her. By not moving she was able to calm herself.

Her body huddled next to his, slowly letting go of the fear that had gripped her like a vise for what seemed forever. Just two weeks ago they were together like this, the last time they'd made love: then the ringing of the phone and Karen's terrible screams at the other end.

She must have conveyed her intense emotional need for him because he pressed her closer, never moving, never pushing or rushing. This was his way.

"You must have known how desperately I needed you tonight," she said quietly.

His answer was to lightly kiss the top of her head as he cradled her to his chest.

"Did you know she was pregnant?"

"Yes. Judy told Karen shortly after we brought her home. One of the few times she talked to Karen. Why?"

"Scooter told Greg and I, but he acted as though he'd just learned about it."

"That's true. He didn't know. Karen only told him after she died."

"What a terrible blow."

"A final irony."

"What did she hope to gain by keeping it a secret?"

"She'd tried to talk Judy into having an abortion. If things had gone the way she'd planned, Scooter would never have known. He didn't need to know. But in the midst of all her grieving, she told him. A double heartbreak for him."

"Sometimes I wonder how he lived with her selfishness all these years."

She became still, this was the first time she'd ever heard him express such vehemence toward Karen. "What did he say?"

"Not much, he just cried. It was terrible to hear. You know, I have to think about my own baby. What if I'd lost Selena, only to learn she was carrying a child, and to lose the child also. A double loss is almost too much to bear."

"What could he have done?"

"Maybe talk her out of her dark thoughts."

"How? She wasn't listening to them about anything."

"She wasn't listening to Karen. She may have listened to her father. He may have been able to convince her that the baby she was carrying was important enough for her to try and save herself."

"I don't know Al, she was pretty low."

Quiet talk in the dark filled the night. "Who would have thought there would be so much pain in our lives, now." Tears were flowing freely. She needed to cry.

"Things happen that we just can't foresee. We made decisions we thought were right for us. Maybe they were at the time, but looking back, the circumstances appear clearer."

She knew his response was as much a personal statement of his own life as an opinion about so many others they knew. Darkness shielded the pain that briefly flickered in his eyes. He shifted, drawing her body partly beneath his.

His lips were near her ear, "We do the best we can."

"But our best doesn't keep us from making mistakes," she said, soaking up the comfort of his body.

Many thoughts crossed her mind, as she lay awake, none of which was more important than her need to be with him. This is real. Right now. Just being here with you is the only important thing. She was quiet, hardly breathing, her thoughts drifting.

"Our lives weren't supposed to be like this," she said.

"True. Some of those old choices weren't so hot, I'll be the first to admit."

She snuggled closer. "We were supposed to go to school, get married, have children, and live happily ever after. We got out of school all right, made lots of money, and we're still waiting to live happily--never mind ever after, just happy in the present would be okay."

"At this moment I'm not concerned about how I might be happier." His lips brushed her ears.

A forlorn sound was her only response. "You've been under a lot of pressure. Let go, relax," he whispered.

The night was a living thing, at once comforting them, but also revealing their vulnerabilities. When she started to talk again, dawn was coloring the sky, shining through the floor-to-ceiling glass. Pent up feelings and emotions could not be contained.

"We have dreams, plans and hopes. The thing is, only a handful of people dream right. Most of us dream about the wrong things. Look at us, you, me, Marva, Karen, and Scooter -- even Greg. Remember our dream time, how we talked endlessly about the big houses we'd have, the cars, fancy schools for our children, money, money, money. For sure we dreamed wrong."

She closed her eyes and went off to a place in her mind where she thought she was alone, but he'd followed her. His head resting on hers as he waited for her to let go; to unburden herself. He knew she was trying to find a way to deal with Judy's death, to understand how their expectations had led to her undoing.

She turned and held him tighter, her nails digging into his flesh. Shifting slightly, she drew one knee higher between his legs. Like always, he gave into her needs, gentling her and calming her, his hands moving over her back, in and out of the narrow indentation of her backbone.

"That was a magical time. A time when we could just go after the dreams we had for ourselves. There was no way to know parts of the dream happen everyday. But for me, somewhere out there was a future where I would stand on top of a pile of things and places, and people."

She raised her head and looked into his face, "Then I could say, I have my dreams. But what I found was the big lie. You, on the other hand, were always your own person. Certainly you're lived out your dreams, haven't you?"

"You can answer that question yourself," he said pulling her head back down on his chest. As he caressed her shoulders, his eyes were fixed on the ceiling. She couldn't see the slight frown on his handsome face.

"No, I can't. Tell me."

He responded by softly caressing her back. When he remained silent, she put her lips to his and briefly kissed him, then laid her head between his chin and shoulder, waiting.

"All I ever wanted was to control as much of my little piece of life as I was able to. Growing up in Memphis, I knew early on what I could and couldn't do. I decided I owned myself and I'd never surrender body and soul to anyone. That was the crux of my dream."

"And you didn't."

"True. For a long time, I thought I hadn't, but one day when I wasn't looking someone else grabbed me, and took a big chunk."

Her heart leaped as she held her breath.

177

"There's not a day that goes by I don't ask myself if I'm doing what's necessary to make real my dream. Sometimes I let go of the whole notion, careful not to take myself too seriously."

The hair on his chest tickled her nipples, absent-mindedly moving towards his side, she rose on her elbows. "What I would have done differently was not get married when I did. My expectations were never realized and of course for that, I can only blame myself. I thought marriage was my next step. Karen had a husband and Marva had marked you, Greg was there and he asked me, so I said yes. We were seeing each other, he was funny, and I liked him and thought the feeling was love. To marry him, seemed the right thing to do."

He threaded his fingers through her hair. "In those days marriage was the right thing for many of us. We could have made worst choices."

"We lived with them."

"Or we walked away."

"Many of our friends did. From the outside most of them appear to live enviable lives, but they've taken on so much garbage, the real people inside have almost disappeared. Look at Jimmy, Thelma said when she first saw him, he was the most dynamic guy she'd ever met, aggressive, going places--and she wanted to go right along with him. Even when we first met them Jimmy had a foreign car, they'd moved from DC into Prince George's County. They were a great couple. He and Thelma had sit-down dinners, really classy."

"He's hardly the same man now."

"No, he's almost batty. All he talks about is how white people have ruined his life. At Karen's house after the funeral, he walked around telling everybody how racist his supervisors were, the games people play. It was embarrassing."

"What really happened with him?"

"He'd been doing so well, but as he moved up, he reached a level and wasn't able to go higher. He tried for promotions, but someone else always got the position, a white person. The last time he tried for one and didn't get the job, he accused them of discrimination."

"What do you think?"

"It's hard to prove. The more sophisticated and complicated the job, the easier it is to find subjective excuses for not giving someone a position.

"He's over the wall now, crying spells. Thelma says he just starts to cry for no apparent reason. Sometimes it lasts for hours. No one wants him around anymore, but he hardly lets Thelma out of his sight, so friends avoid her too."

"Sounds like he needs serious help."

"True."

Judy's death had made her more thoughtful. Until tonight she'd kept her grief and resulting thoughts to herself. Now she just wanted to talk, to unburden herself. Images flashed through her mind, old friends, good times, her grandmother's dear face, the cramped apartment on Gerard Street, Johnny's birth.

"I was thinking about the night Johnny was born. I had the impression when I first opened my eyes in the recovery room, that Greg didn't look as happy as he should have at the birth of his son. You were there, was he excited?"

If she'd asked this question last year, his answer would have been different. Tonight, however, there was no need for circumspection. "I can't recall Greg's emotion at the time. My own feelings are what I remember most about that Friday night." His eyes were still focused on the ceiling, but he too, was remembering a night many years ago. "There I was, standing next to one of my best buddies as he welcomed his first born into the world, and all I could think was, this baby should have been mine."

"Oh, Al, how could we not know at the very beginning what we wanted, what we needed?"

"If we'd had crystal balls to read the future, our mistakes and missteps could have been avoided. But there was no way to predict what was to come. Think how different life would be now if Karen and Scooter had known where Judy was headed? She'd be alive today."

"I keep thinking over and over, her life didn't have to be that way. They have everything, yet they are alone, without their children."

Her fingers moved gently over his face, lovingly following the outline of his lips.

"Since her death I've asked myself, what happened. She was the sweetest little girl."

"Before she left for Grayson College Karen tried to talk her into straightening her hair, but, she refused. One of the few times she had the nerve to resist something her mother wanted."

"What I recall is the silly reason they selected Grayson for her. She wanted to go to Howard, but it wasn't good enough until she failed. How the hell can a school that gave her father the capability to let her mother live like a queen, be so bad?"

"You know that was Karen's idea, and she hardly lasted a year."

"Enter Mr. Peter."

"Karen maintains if she'd never gone to Howard, she would never have met him."

"Maybe, maybe not. But, a school can't be blamed for the insecurities Judy brought with her."

"Now, we'll never know."

"Dead and gone from her parents forever. Could the same circumstances have claimed one of our children?"

"I don't know. I would like to think not. But we have to wonder what factors drive young people to such extremes?"

"Children like ours?"

"Children with all the advantages that we gave them."

"But what about the things we left out--what didn't we give them that we should have? Judy didn't know how to feel good about herself. She never learned how to fight back against Karen's domineering ways and constant criticism."

"She tried so hard to please her, but never did, so she just stopped trying." Heleena sat up and drew her knees up to her chin, hugging the sheet around her legs. "I worry so about Richie. I don't know if I did the right thing, sending him to live with Greg."

Not wanting to be separated from her, he too, sat up, wrapping his arms around her. She could feel the steady beat of his heart down the length of her back.

"Sweetheart don't compare the negative way Karen raised her children with the care and concern you used with your own. They're good kids, you don't have to worry about them. They'll be okay."

She leaned back, pressing into him turning her raised lips to meet his. "I love you so," she whispered.

* * *

Two hours later, they were still together, talking quietly.

"You're not alone in being concerned about your children. This thing with Selena has unsettled me more than I like to admit. I'm of two minds. I want her happiness, but I think she's moving too fast. On the other hand, I don't want to be responsible for a decision that might adversely impact her future."

"She's so determined, I don't see how you can stop her from moving in with him."

"I can't really and that is the frustrating part. Who can say what two people mean to each other more than the two people themselves. Still, I think their relationship is not one of substance."

"Maybe they will find this for themselves only by living together. Sometimes that's the only way to know. Are you sure your resistance has more to do with your baby sleeping with a man, than her not being ready for a serious relationship?"

"No, I'm not sure."

"Dr. Harris, I'm shocked. You're showing signs of prudishness," she said in mock severity.

"Sorting out my feelings is tough."

"Its funny how we forget the emotional turmoil surrounding our youthful romances."

"My sister would never have rebelled against my mother, to live with a man."

"Different time, different people."

"Listen baby, I look at my own life and painfully know what can happen when you think you are doing the right thing -- common sense lost among emotions. You'd be mine today if someone had told me to think about what I was doing."

"Life was a little more black and white then."

"It's a fair enough excuse. We can't go on like this, we can't go back, I won't go back. We should have had these years together-- good and bad times, shared."

She sensed his breathing quicken and nestled into him.

When she lapsed into silence, he gently probed, "Hasn't it crossed your mind, you and me?"

She was so overcome with emotion; she didn't trust herself to speak. Instead she rolled over, put a hand on each side of his head and kissed him with desperate passion. When she lifted her head she saw the pain in his eyes, and the love. They hadn't talked about where their relationship was taking them, but she should have known he was thinking about this.

She'd been content to have him with her at his convenience, thinking those times were enough to satisfy her. Now she'd have to discuss the reality of their relationship with him. For the first time in their long friendship, she was scared, afraid of what might lay ahead.

He gently coaxed her with a kiss.

"No. I haven't permitted myself. I'm frightened. You mean too much to me. I don't even want to consider the possibility that you'd take your friendship from me."

"And my love?"

"Oh Al, it's too scary to think about."

"Sweetheart, I'm not talking about taking anything away from you. You and I have, over the years, discussed everything under the sun and now we need to talk about us."

"Al, I am happy with the way things are between us."

"There's that word again, what do you mean by happy?"

She started to tremble. He covered her body with his, comforting her. "Sweetheart, I didn't mean to upset you."

"Just hold me. Please, I can't talk about this right now, please."

He kissed her cheek, now wet with tears and felt the fast beat of her heart.

Finally, she exhaled deeply, "I can't bear to think that you have had enough of me."

"If I lived a hundred years, I could never get enough of you, so don't…"

"I have to believe you, but I want us to stay as we are. I'm afraid of what change could do to us."

"Our relationship has already undergone total change. My feelings for you didn't just spring alive two months ago. Although I'm not one who believes in love at first sight, you have been precious to me almost from the time we met. For twenty-five years my love for you has grown steadily."

Still holding her head so he looked directly into her eyes, he prevented her from turning away. "Open your eyes, sweetheart look at me." He kissed her deeply, then lightly touched his lips to her eyelids and cheeks. "Didn't you know baby? Didn't you know my feelings for you?"

His head lay next to hers now, so her lips touched his ear lobe as she answered. "My first inclination is to say no. Lately, however, I've reached deep, trying to be honest with myself. Did I see signs? I don't know. I was always so comfortable with you. You were my anchor and my best friend, the first person I think about in any situation."

"And that has not changed."

"I know, but the night I really knew there was more, was the night we first made love. There are so many images that come to mind. Remember that New Year's Eve party at Karen and Scooter's when it snowed so much they hired someone to clean the street right up to their house?"

"Who could forget it?"

"Well, that night, I felt something I've recalled lately. You always look great, but that night you were so strikingly handsome, I wanted to touch you, connect with you." She hesitated. "I'm having trouble explaining my feelings."

"Go on, tell me as best you can remember."

"I felt an intense attraction to you. I was never shy about asking you or Scooter to dance with me. But that night I hesitated, waited for you to ask me. In your arms I experienced emotions that were disturbing. I wondered what it would be like to have you make love to me. The thought was so shocking I felt a terrible shame. But my mind kept returning to the same idea -- how love would be with you. The thought attracted me and repelled me at the same time. Of course, I considered it no more than sexual arousal. After all, I hadn't been with a man since Greg left. At that time, two years had passed."

She closed her eyes, turning the pages of her memory, Leatha's warning hovering, like a deadly snake, how could you not know.

There was never any question in my mind that you would not be there for me. I called you when I wanted to, I was free to call on you at your office and there was never a problem when I picked up the phone and asked Marva to speak with you. I grew to believe I had rights to your time and attention. Is that why the physical relationship is so easy to accept? Her mind looked back.

What you have given me is much more than I should expect, but I'm not ready to let go, I will not let you go, this little part of you is mine; I'm not hurting anyone. A hush settled in the room as Leatha's warning intruded on the night. This time her face appeared across the room next to Mr. Wilson, with his grotesque ebony face. Their mocking looks only made her cling tighter.

"Put a pin in it," he told her, "We'll talk further some other time." It was clear to him she was not ready for more discussion of their situation.

"Thanks"

"What are your plans for tomorrow?"

"I'll spend time with Karen. She's slowly coming to grips with her loss, but there's a growing anger in her and she's directing it against Scooter. They are not sharing their sorrow. I sure hope this tragedy doesn't drive a wedge between them."

"She's tested him to the max. Sometimes I think he's a glutton for punishment."

"Have you had a chance to spend anytime alone with him since the funeral, just the two of you?"

"Last Thursday."

"How did he seem to you?"

"Sad, very sad. His work will help. When we were together, he talked mostly about Judy and Junior. He mourns the fact that he missed so much of their childhoods."

"We all did. There was no way around it."

"But the loss stands out more when you know there will never be a chance to make up the time lost during childhood. Anyway, I suggested he take off for a couple of weeks, get away with Karen and grieve."

"What did he say?"

"His patients need him. They'll get away later. He says his work takes his mind off his grief. Scooter's like that, totally dedicated. He's the best and his patients come first."

"Right after Karen."

"Everything is right after Karen, but his absolute dedication is something I've always envied."

"You're kidding."

"No, his reason for going into medicine was because he genuinely enjoys people and the desire to work for them. Scooter's the kind of person who loves to give himself. Believe me, not everyone enters our profession with an idea of serving people."

"That certainty doesn't apply to you."

"I enjoy my work, but I went into medicine because the profession would give me independence."

"I don't believe that."

"It's true."

"Al, I've never heard you say that before. Knowing how hard you work makes it difficult to believe."

"Believe me sweetheart, I love what I do, but if times were different, I would have chosen a career in music."

"Did you even seriously consider music?"

"No, too chancy. Mama would never let me forget how hard life would be trying to make a living, singing and playing the piano. I enjoyed music so, she once said, she was sorry she'd kept the piano."

"Why?"

"She wasn't sure whether I'd take my chances in the music business or go to college. Around Memphis it was easy to be seduced into joining one of hundreds of groups that were trying to make the big time. My aunt, my dad's sister lived with us for a while and she left the piano when she moved. I started playing, began lessons and found I was pretty good."

"What about singing lessons?"

"Nope. That came later, just something I did along with my piano playing."

"This is amazing, as long as I've known you, I never knew this bit of history."

"Now you know everything?"

The time was 4:00 a.m.; she fought the creeping drowsiness by shifting positions, again needing to take full advantage of the security of his body. He lay still until she found the position she wanted, then folded her in his arms as she placed her head on his chest. Unable to stay awake any longer, she was soon sleeping quietly.

When she awoke hours later and raised herself, his eyes were already open. "Hi, sleepy head, I thought you'd sleep the morning away."

"No, I tried not to fall asleep at all. It just slipped up on me."

"You needed the rest."

When he left she took a cup of the coffee she'd brewed for them and went out the small morning room at the end of the family room. Sipping the hot liquid, she suddenly realized, they'd spent the night together, talking and holding each other, and never even made love.

SEPTEMBER-OCTOBER

Chapter 15

Judy was buried six weeks ago, but they were still gripped by the shock of her death. Heleena reserved two weeks in St. Maartin. Carl owned a place on the island and offered it to them for as long as they wanted. When she and Marva put the plan to Karen she accepted immediately. Since the funeral, she'd languished at home, fighting with Scooter, reliving Judy's last unhappy months.

They'd connect with Marva in Miami. She was flying from Birmingham.

Just the ride from the airport lifted Karen's spirits. She made jokes with the porter who brought their bags upstairs.

Their corner unit had ocean views from both sides and the pool below. Tropical hues dominated the decor, peach and sand, mixed with pale blue. The all-purpose living room and largest bedroom opened onto balconies.

The porter opened the sliding glass doors and they savored the warm ocean breezes. Within hours they were on the road to the neighborhood food center, enjoying the sun and looking forward to fourteen carefree days.

By the third day they were attuned to the island's easy pace. As they sat in the warm sun chatting about nothing and everything, the blue-green water of the ocean rolled ashore in its eternal ebb and flow, like life. Their chairs sat on a small rise, directly in front of an old windswept sea grape tree.

"Hey kiddo, you've got some of your color back," Marva said to Karen.

She did look better and more alive since their arrival. That pale yellow had taken on a peachy blush. The sun had quickly marked them. Marva was tanned and very pretty. Heleena who was the darkest of the three simply glowed. The dark brown of her hair seemed to shine with reddish highlights. Three beautiful women and not one of them looked her age.

Beach boys roaming the sliver of sand hawking supposedly gold necklaces and other junk constantly barraged them. They waved each away in turn.

"Why do they let these guys on the beach? As much money as we paid, there's no reason we should have to be bothered with them," Karen said while putting sunscreen oil on her legs. As always, she thought money was the key to anything. Even someone else's money.

Heleena financed this entire jaunt. She made all the arrangements, so great her desire that they be together. As she sat staring out across the water that unaccounted for fear started again in the pit of her stomach. Unexplainable, the emotions had dogged her all summer -- an old premonition of disaster. But certainly not anymore, disaster had come and gone. So why this feeling in such a beautiful place?

"Hey girl, where've you gone off to?" Marva said, looking at her.

"Nowhere, just thinking."

"She's been doing that all summer." Karen said.

"Thinking about what?" Marva probed.

"No secrets."

They laughed together knowing what that meant. When they were young marrieds, they used to discuss everything about being married. If they thought someone was holding back, they'd say "No secrets" and the accused party had to come clean with all the details.

"I'm happy we're together again, you know, just us, no children. Oh, baby I'm sorry, I didn't mean that." She reached for Karen and hugged her tightly.

"I know what you mean, girl time like in the old no secrets days".

"And no husbands," Marva said, oblivious to the interchange between Heleena and Karen. Heleena looked at her over the top of her dark glasses, but said nothing. Karen gave her a long questioning look. Instead she said, "Remember the first time we came down here and brought the kids."

"Hell yes, I remember," Marva said. "Al spent all his time playing with Selena. There were few romantic moments for us."

"He's spoiled her, and who knows that better than you?"

"They had such a good time, though -- and the sun turned my baby into a little brown doll," Karen said.

Heleena held her breath, knowing painful memories would crop up in any conversation they had. That's why they'd come, to give her a chance to grieve and remember. They were silent for a few minutes, unsure where the conversation was headed, waiting, prepared to take the ball and run with it in whatever direction Karen chose.

Roused by a woman selling tee shirts, three for ten dollars, they needed to divert their attention in another direction just now.

"I'll buy four for twelve dollars," Marva told the woman.

"Four for thirteen, the woman countered. That's my cost, but for you I sell that price."

"Twelve fifty," Marva went on, enjoying the bartering.

Not to be out done, the women quickly came back, "Twelve seventy-five," and began laying the shirts in front of Marva for her inspection.

"I'll get one for mama, Alva, mama's friend, Mrs. Emma, and Selena, if she want's one. She's so peculiar these days."

She held two of them up for closer inspection.

"What about this one?" she asked, holding up a big white shirt with blue letters across the front which read, "If you don't stop, all this sex is gonna kill you...Lay me out in bronze casket then."

"Its' cute", she said, "but I don't know anyone who can stand that one."

"What about you ladies?" she said looking at Heleena and Karen.

"Oh, I haven't decided if I want tee shirts. Will you be on the beach tomorrow?"

"Yes, I come everyday."

"Check with me tomorrow. Okay?"

"I will. You ladies have a nice day." She put away her money and turned to walk away.

"Thank you, we're trying."

The young girls strolled up and down the beach, their supple smooth bodies tanned like toast. They drew admiring glances from one and all. Scattered about were a few who swam and sunbathed topless. They wore about them a certain disdain for all whose breasts no longer had the pert upturn nipples that reached for the kiss of the sun. They were beautiful and knew it -- admired by some, envied by others. Hair streaked colors ranging from palest gold to deepest red and burnished brown.

The old biddies strolled too, in one-piece swimsuits, mostly black. They walked with their husbands, wrinkled chests and bellies, some with nitro patches, gravity working everywhere. Marva, who still looked damn fine in her two-piece swimsuit waded into the surf, then slipped under, swimming effortlessly.

"What's wrong with her? There's something going on. She sounds a tad bit angry," Karen said, not turning her head.

Heleena's stomach did an automatic flip, "Beats me. She's been acting strange since May."

She looked directly at Heleena, who was staring out to sea, "And you don't know why?"

"Uh, Uh."

"Well, this is a no secrets trip, we'll talk tonight."

"Don't push her."

"I won't. So what's on tap for this afternoon?"

"Phillipsburg."

"Good old Front Street, huh?"

"Yep. A zillion shops."

"Are you looking for anything in particular?"

"No. I'll just look around. If anything catches my fancy, I may be interested. No matter, I always look at the gold trinkets anyway."

"Remember those gold bangles you brought the girls, the first time we left them at home?"

"Yes, and did they love them. Anne still wears hers every single day."

"My baby wore hers for a long time, then she stopped. For almost two years, she never put them on, she just wore glass beads, junk."

Heleena remembered the last time Judy came to her house. She wore the bracelets that day. "Most young girls prefer the handmade beaded necklaces and bracelets."

"But, you know what? When we found her, she had them on." Her voice caught, but Heleena didn't attempt to stop her.

"I didn't think anything of it at first. But, it has to mean something. Don't you think so?"

"Absolutely."

"Once my baby made her decision she wanted me to know she still loved me."

"Sweetheart she never stopped loving you. Always believe that."

"Heleena, our relationship became such a tug of war, she just stopped coming home, and whenever she did, she stayed in her room. What hurts most is that the only times, during this last year that I saw her happy, were the times she came home after being with that scum." She wiped her eyes with the end of the towel.

"There is nothing rational about the way we love--or who. The person who figures that out can buy the world."

"But we weren't like that. We fell in love with men who,..." she waved her hands in the air trying to find the right words.

"Men we thought would make life easy for us?"

"Well, yes, men who had futures."

"Moneyed futures."

"Right. Nothing wrong with that, we've been able to have everything in life we wanted."

"But did it make us happy, truly happy?"

"Who worries about happiness at our ages?" Marva came up behind them. She'd swam to the end of the beach and walked back at an angle which brought her to the rear of where they sat.

"The question is, did we marry for love?" Karen asked.

"Or money?" Heleena added.

"Hey, are we going for the real deal?"

"What do you think?" Karen wanted to know. "With big Al, was it love or money?"

Heleena stared straight ahead, her eyes focused on the blue-green horizon.

"I have to think about that answer, real hard. What about Scooter? Was it love, his money, or his looks?" They all laughed, knowing her answer.

"Strike looks, fast."

"Uh, huh," Marva continued, "love?"

"Ohm, probably, somewhat."

"Money?" she asked accusingly.

"For sure."

"But he didn't have any then."

"Oh, but it was a certainty he would and very soon after school."

"How did we get on this topic anyway?"

"You know when we talk, one thing leads to another and eventually we've discussed everything under the sun," Heleena said rejoining the conversation. "We started out reminiscing on affairs of the heart and the mysteries involved."

"And they are indeed mysterious," Marva said.

"So Marva, you bagged Prince, the old fashion way. A sure-fire move during our time," Karen said, laughing.

"That's a joke, nobody bags Prince Al, he's a force unto himself."

"Ah, come on kiddo, there was many a woman out there trying to get him, but as my granddad would say, you reeled in the big one, the prize."

"At one time I thought so too."

"Marva, *paleez*," Heleena couldn't contain herself.

"Hey, I think we're on to something. What do you think?" Karen asked, turning to Heleena.

There was no need to reply. There was definitely something happening with Marva and they would know about it soon enough.

The sun was directly overhead now, but they were protected by the jaunty caps purchased in the shop across the street from the hotel.

"Think we ought to go in? The sun's coming down like hell fire." Since she didn't go into the water, Heleena had no relief from the constant heat, even under the big umbrella.

"No, the sun feels good. Lets stay awhile longer," Karen said.

"Sure? You'd better be careful you don't burn."

"Don't worry, I'm protected. I used the strongest sun blocker they had in the store."

"Good enough, we just don't want you to get a burn on top of everything else," Marva said.

"I don't know how I would have lived through these last weeks without you guys."

"Remember, right after Heleena came back from her honeymoon in Nassau, and we got together to celebrate?"

"Sure, I remember," Karen said, "How can we forget, we celebrated so hard, we had to send for our husbands to take us home."

"Also, remember what we promised each other?"

"Yes."

"We would share everything--the bad times as well as the good."

"And we have," Heleena said. "If it hadn't been for you two and Al and Scooter, I would have had no social life after Greg left."

"Not so, we can name a few guys who were interested. Divorce put a lot of ex-wives on the shelf, but you really didn't need to lean on us."

"I don't know. No one was beating down my door."

"Heleena, you could have any one you want, but for one little problem."

"What's that?"

They'd changed positions and were now sitting in a circle, facing each other.

"No, the question is who?" Marva said.

"Who, then?"

"My husband, that's who."

The ringing in her ears and the tremors in her lower abdomen made Heleena feel sick. The ocean waves which were so calm just minutes before now caused dizziness. Behind the dark glasses, no one could see her distress. Outwardly she was still as a statue.

Unknowingly, Karen came to her rescue. "What does Al have to do with anything?"

"Heleena allows him to pass judgment on any man who crosses her path and he takes the task too seriously."

"There are dogs out there," Karen said. "If a woman can get any inside information, she's way ahead of the game."

"I don't question him about every man I see. Anyway, there is no hoard of men looking for me."

"That might be true, but you tell me, has Al ever told you that Mr. so-and-so is a good catch, go for him? Think. Has he ever given you a positive answer"?

"I sometimes mention a particular guy and ask Al if he knows him--that is all."

"But, has he ever told you anything positive?"

Karen pulled her glasses low on her nose so she could see Heleena clearly. "No secrets, remember."

"Well, not exactly."

"Hey, I rest my case."

"Marva, Al's always exercised good judgment, hasn't he?" Karen asked her directly.

"His judgment isn't the issue here. His self-righteous attitude where Heleena is concerned is the problem for her."

"That's fine for you to say. You took the cream right off the top when you snagged Al. So you can sit here and make light of Heleena's situation."

"I'm not making light of her condition," she said looking at Heleena. "Its just that if you ever expect to get into a relationship don't rely on Al so much. Anyway, you all have a tendency to attribute perfection to Al. He's not perfect you know."

"So tell us," Karen pushed her. "No secrets remember?"

Marva sat back in her lounge chair and put both arms above her head, looking out to sea like she was looking for the right words. "He's different now, kind of withdrawn. We don't talk much anymore we..."

"You've been away for most of the last three months," Karen interrupted.

"True, but its more than that. Time is slipping away. Now I feel like I'm Marva Harris living with a man whose name happens to be Alvin R. Harris."

Heleena listened intently. She knew she'd better say something soon before they noticed her silence.

"They say that happens sometimes when couples have been married a long time--a stage they often go through."

"No, it's deeper than that. We're pulling apart."

Heleena's internal voice responded. I'm sure not the reason. Our relationship is no more demanding on your marriage than before. I don't see Al anymore now than I did six months ago, or even a year ago. He is a good husband to you.

"What do you mean?" Karen asked.

"Karen, you and Scooter have been married as long as I have."

"Longer."

"Well, you must have had the feeling at some point, that you and Scooter were just not clicking? That something was off center?"

"Since my baby went away I feel a distance from him, a feeling I never had before. When I met him, I knew Scooter was the man to make all my dreams come true and he promised me he would."

"And he has done everything in his power to keep his promise," Heleena added.

"Without a doubt," Karen agreed.

"What about you Heleena. When you and Greg were together? No secrets."

"There are no secrets about Greg and me. We were mismatched from day one."

"You're right, no secrets there. When you all first announced your engagement, that's what Al said to me. Even though Greg is one of his best friends, when the split came he was not surprised. But anyway, getting back to my original question. Even in the mismatch, were there times when you couldn't make anything work?"

"To tell you the truth Marva, I hadn't a clue about the inner workings of marriage except that I had a husband. You and Karen seemed to have hit pay dirt, so I thought I must have too. My career and the children kept my mind from ever dwelling on whether I was happy or even how to measure marital bliss. I just didn't know."

"And sex, was that good with Greg?"

"I've...," she stopped dead. She was about to say, I've had better.

"Go on," Marva urged her.

"Whatever I did or did not have with Greg is a dead and buried issue--no longer important."

Karen sat up, removed her glasses and asked Marva, "Tell us once and for all, how's sex with the Prince? We can only imagine what it must be like to sleep with him every night, huh?"

As jittery as she felt, Heleena found that question laughable. She and Marva could testify on that point.

"Go ahead, no holding back. I want to hear this." Karen was pushing harder.

Marva released a deep, to-the-heart sigh, before she answered. "Sex with Al is good, but he's always held something back, when we're together."

Karen and Heleena waited. Marva's tone indicated there was more.

"He never just lets go to the point that I have every part of him, for the moment, at least."

"Does he satisfy you?" Karen would not let go.

"He satisfies me as far as sex is concerned, but he doesn't make love to me. There's a difference. I'm not getting what I ought to get from him. And I've been wondering lately if I can talk to him about the way I feel. Then again I'm not sure if I want to talk to him about this. I'm not sure I can even put these feelings into words."

Helena retreated into her thoughts. His heart beats with mine every time--and the way his mouth catches my last breath-- folding into him--the blood coursing through his veins until the surging flow rises cascading through me--giving all, keeping nothing.

"How long has this been bothering you?"

"Being away from home most of the summer has given me time to reflect on my personal life and work life. I don't know if I told you, but I told Heleena, I'm thinking about not going back to the D.C. Government."

"You're retiring?"

"I don't have the age to retire. I may just walk away."

"What will you do?"

"I haven't the faintest idea, maybe nothing."

"Now is the time for you to do what you enjoy. Something just to please yourself, not Al nor Selena." Heleena was sincere in her encouragement. "You've always loved beautiful jewelry. Maybe you can work that into a business."

"I'd probably end up keeping all the inventory for myself, but the idea is worth considering. Girl you're always right on time."

"You can pick up a few pieces on Front Street."

"You're right. The first place I'll look is the little shop where Al bought my diamond bracelet."

"You never wear that anymore."

"It's too dangerous now to wear diamonds in public. I'd get myself killed just for a nice piece of jewelry. Wearing an expensive bracelet like that is just asking for trouble."

"Well wear it at home."

"What's the purpose of having a five caret diamond bracelet if no one knows?" Karen added. "But, you can wear it for your husband-- just the bracelet. Get my meaning, bracelet and birthday suit. That ought to get you two more."

"Since you're bringing up now days, I'll just say this, the birthday suit shit, doesn't work the same way it once did."

"No?"

"No, and stop looking over your glasses at me, as though there is some mystery."

"Well, is there?"

"Of course not."

"If you say so."

Heleena rose, gathering her things. "I'm going in to shower and relax a little before supper."

Marva looked at her watch. "Four-o'clock already. One more swim then I'll be ready to go in, too. What about you?" she asked Karen.

"I'll wait for you."

* * *

As they dressed, they moved back and forth from bedrooms to the baths leaving pieces of clothing in their wake. This was a vacation, do nothing time, and they'd arranged to have maid service every day so there was little incentive in spending precious time keeping the apartment neat. Three clotheshorses caused quite a mess.

To their surprise, Karen was the first to announce, ready. The lime green sundress she'd chosen was a designer original. It didn't fit as snug as it had when she brought it at the beginning of summer.

They had 7:30 P.M. reservations at Port-de-Plaza, the Friday night seafood buffet.

"Ready?" Heleena called out ten minutes later. She was standing by the door, keys in hand. They'd rented a neat little compact which the doorman permitted them to park near the entrance. As she did each time they went out Heleena passed him a five-dollar bill. She was sleek in a white linen dress with straps crossing in the back. Marva wore a black sleeveless organza dress with a flared skirt.

Even on a resort island where the sand, sun and sea added mightily to the healthy good looks of all inhabitants, these three made a stunning appearance when they entered the elegant restaurant twenty minutes later. They were like young girls enjoying themselves, oblivious to the admiring glances all around.

Across the room sat a young couple, thirtyish maybe, very much in love.

"Quite a place to be in love, huh?" Marva commented, nodding in their direction.

"Any place will do when two people love each other," Heleena said.

"Still, this is a very romantic island, sail boats in the distance, waves crashing on the shore, far away from home and the mundane," Marva, said bent on defending her position.

"So much for love and romance. We're here with each other for company and companionship. If we'd wanted romance, we would have brought our men," Karen reminded them.

"Just an observation, no big deal," Marva responded.

Chapter 16

Even though the summer heat held on longer than usual, the days were moving too fast. Eventually she'd have to answer Al's question, "What about us?"

She wasn't ready to have the discussion yet. Not that it hadn't occupied most of her waking hours. It had.

She'd started to look forward to seeing him, often. With great restraint she behaved as normal as possible. Whenever, they were together, unless they were alone, she was careful not to reach out and touch him as they talked, which she would normally do.

Her touch was different now, a lover's touch, more like a caress. She was afraid someone would notice the difference.

He was responding differently to her also, more subdued. No words were spoken about this change, but they knew. The touch of one's love is softer, gentler, a lingering promise of more to follow.

In passion his dark brown eyes mesmerized her. The pupils seeming to change colors, opening, the very center of the iris slowly fading into a hint of darkest night. The first time she saw it, she was drawn as if swallowed by a tidal wave. Later, when he caught her staring, he wanted to know, "What's wrong?"

"I never knew your eyes changed colors," she'd replied.

"They don't."

"Sometimes."

With her he let go everything and the changing shadows always emerged.

* * *

Marva was of two minds. Driven by excitement she hadn't felt in years caused her to take this chance, even as hope that her life with Al might improve, slowly faded.

Not once this summer was he bothered that she was spending so much time in Alabama. He doesn't miss me, and frankly, I don't miss his coldness.

Her too long-suffering attitude had turned to anger. They'd hardly made love this summer. Not at all the last time she was at home. The time before the funeral she'd felt it was only because she'd pushed, that he'd performed his husbandly duties.

This was so unlike him. Even when she'd suspected there were other women he never let up on their physical relationship. He was the same person with the same appetites, only now he was consciously holding himself back from her. "So why shouldn't I find a little comfort, enjoy Oscar's friendship and company.

Although Oscar had come by her mother's house twice, even having dinner with them, this was the third time she'd made the trip to Montgomery. Tonight she was anxious and overly concerned that she look her best. She needn't worry on that score, she'd retained all of her good looks. The burnished glow she brought back from the Caribbean gave her the look of a young girl who'd played, carefree in the sun all summer.

She needed to put death out of her mind. Tonight was for time-out. A few hours with an old friend, but one whose company she enjoyed more and more. And it was obvious he was not about to let go of this renewed contact with her. He actually seemed flattered by her attention. The years had been kind to him. Even his receding hairline enhanced his mellow look.

Tonight they were getting together with a small group of friends and classmates at one of the couple's home. She'd return to her mother's house tomorrow. The distance was too far to drive back tonight.

* * *

As she did everyday now, Karen counted the days since Judy's death. She always performed this rite in secret, in her baby's room. Forty-nine days now.

The first thing she did every morning was come to this room. When her husband had asked why, she'd simply replied, "I need to." The truth is, she used the room as a place to think. To sort through the feelings and emotions filling her head.

All her agony over how Judy lived her life was losing none of its pull over her, but now the emptiness caused by her loss demanded refilling. Karen's world was defined by her ability to spend limitless sums on her possessions including her children, but one, and then the other, had left her. She was forced to look at her life. At long last she realized she didn't like what she saw, and the road ahead was unfamiliar.

During these quiet moments every morning she found there was a certain excitement building within her. Excitement she kept to herself. Even during the day when she wanted clear thinking she came here. She concentrated on these burgeoning emotions, giving little thought to Scooter's grief.

There were changes coming in her life. And soon. Except for this special corner in the house, there was no peace for her. She'd made up her mind she needed some space from Scooter. He must have sensed her feelings because lately he too, was distant.

She moved from bed to window, no longer touching the many dolls that sat together in little groups around the room. Minutes later she left the room, carefully closing the door.

This morning she went into her son's bedroom. It too, was a perfect sanctuary. Only here there were toy trains and trucks, instead of dolls. She touched them in turn, sat on the bed then walked out.

Downstairs, everything in the opulent living room stood like trophies before her. She went around touching each piece of furniture. The tall glass curio cabinet contained a complete collection of black Llardro figures. Standing directly in front of the locked doors she carefully looked at each piece, remembering how it came to her. The Dancer had been given to her by Scooter and the children one Mother's Day. Heleena gave her the baseball boy she'd bought in St. Maartin, and the seated girl purchased in Nassau. She bought the others herself, usually at a time she needed a quick pick-me-up.

Today, however, they stirred none of the exuberance she'd felt upon acquiring these expensive icons. They were just ceramics.

During the previous two weeks, she'd gradually come to the decision, which she now acknowledged by stating out loud. "I'm leaving."

There was no one to hear her, but she surprised herself. Simply because, instead of coming to grips with her loss, accepting it, she'd stoked the fires, wearing her grief like a mantle. But the immersion had freed her to at least consider the road ahead, painful though it may be.

She didn't quite understand what was happening to her. But, a professional would surely tell her she had started the process of letting go, saying goodbye and picking up the pieces that were left.

* * *

He'd dropped ten pounds, which wasn't hard, he needed to get rid of the extra weight, but his cheeks were sunken, making him look haggard. His glasses needed adjusting. They kept slipping down his nose. And his hair had taken on that look of neglect, which is a true sign that a man has started to disassemble. For the first time the thin patches over his scalp were noticeable. The tight beads clumped together.

As was customary for him, he worked all day in his office, doing the fine job he'd always done. But, there was a change. He became so focused on individual tasks that he was lost to anything else going on around him. A mind doctor would say he was trying to block out that part of his world too painful for consideration.

Karen did notice how badly his clothes fit and she said so. "Why don't we go out next Saturday and get you some new clothes."

Surprised, he agreed. She was different lately. More serious. She'd never paid any attention to the clothes he wore. Why now?

"If you haven't any other plans, I'll take you out to dinner. Just the two of us."

"It's been a long time since we've done that."

"Too long," he said, "We must start living again."

The emotions she'd always stirred in him still ruffled his heart. But now she needed him--they needed each other to sort through the after shocks of their tragedy.

* * *

Al decided Heleena was his. He didn't have to play with the decision. So, now he had to plan for them.

That small place she'd occupied in his heart, which had burned steadily all these years, was now a flame that could no longer be contained. Fate would not take her from him again.

Tonight he waited in his office for her. Selena made him promise to discuss their differences with her.

She rang the doorbell shortly after six. His plan was for them to go out to dinner with Selena and talk her out of the determined intention to move in with her boyfriend.

Heleena was splendid as usual, wearing a green and white checked linen suit. Because of the heat she wore her hair in a soft bun at the nape of her neck. A single pearl stud adorned each ear. Her smile was the only greeting he needed.

"You're earlier than I expected."

"I wanted to get here before Selena. Is there anything new I should know before we meet her?"

"Nothing's changed," he said locking the door and following her up the stairs.

She sat on the couch and he sat across from her on the other side of the coffee table.

"Where are we eating"?

"I told Selena to pick a place. She's supposed to call and let me know."

They were comfortable companions. Heleena removed her pumps and leaned on the sofa arm with her feet tucked under her hips. Her jacket lay across the back of the sofa and the creamy lace camisole gave her a fresh, soft look.

"Under what conditions would you consent and let her move in with her guy?"

"It's no good."

She gracefully rose from the sofa, moved around the table and stood behind his chair, hands on his shoulders. He leaned back.

"This is what young people do now. They want to be together, to show commitment. Don't you remember those emotions?" She massaged the tight muscles running from his neck across his shoulders.

His long fingers covered her hands, stilling the soothing touch. "I'm surprised you should ask me such a question. I was committed, absent the emotions."

Withdrawing her hands she now came around and sat on the edge of the table, leaning very close. "Sometimes we forget the strong emotions the young have when they're in love. But, when we honestly recall those powerful moments in our own lives, they're no different from what our children feel. You must remember."

"I'll tell you what I do remember. I remember wanting to do what all young men wanted, to bed every girl I could. Of course there were precious few available in those days, but the thought hardly ever left my mind."

"So, you can't bear the thought of Selena's boyfriend feeling just as you did? Do you honestly believe they are waiting to move in together before the physical expression of their love?"

He smiled and shook his head. "But I don't have to like the idea."

"That's fine." She lifted his hand to her lips and kissed it. Just as she moved to return to the sofa, the phone rang.

It was Selena.

"You won't be able to make it at all?"

"She's sitting here and yes we've discussed it. She's leaning toward your position."

"Sure." He passed the phone to Heleena.

"Hi."

"You convinced him?" she asked.

"Maybe. I'm still working on him."

"Thank you, thank you, thank you."

"Talk to you later. Love you."

Al was standing, hands in his pocket. "I guess my baby is no baby anymore."

"No. She's a young woman now. Let her enjoy this time in her life. It passes too quickly."

He sat next to her on the sofa.

"It's just the two of us now, where do you want to eat?"

"You decide. It doesn't matter to me. I'm really not all that hungry."

"I'll send out for something."

Ms. Hawkins' church sold dinners every Friday and he'd always supported the endeavor by purchasing fifteen to twenty every week. They were donated to a senior citizens home run by her church. Tonight he ordered two to be sent to his office.

By the time the food arrived neither was very hungry. They picked at the food, fried fish, potato salad, greens and cornbread.

Heleena had taken the combs from her hair. She'd started to wilt. But, because she enjoyed being with him so much, she was reluctant to leave.

She'd never seen him so agitated. "She'll do what is right," she tried to assure him.

"I don't want her to get herself into a trap that she'll regret for the rest of her life. What appears reasonable now, years down the road can become like a stone around her neck. Believe me, I know what I'm talking about."

And she did. He was clearly annoyed. He'd always been there for her and she wanted to offer him some assurance that things would work out for Selena. But how could she? What words would allay his fears? The emotional bonds in relationships between men and women were not always based in reality and, of course, they carried risks.

The only comfort she could give him was herself. So she reached out, drew him to her and pressed her mouth to the side of his neck. The rush of his blood vibrated against her lips as it flowed in an angry stream.

She whispered, "Have confidence in her." Slowly she moved her mouth around his cheek to his lips.

Soon he rose from the sofa and walked to the window, his back to her. "If she makes a mistake now, she'll have to live with it for the rest of her life."

"Would you feel differently if she were interested in another guy-- someone more to your liking?"

He turned to face her, hands in his pants pockets. "I've asked myself that question and I honestly can't say that would make a difference. What does she know about life and love and relationships?"

"As much as we did at twenty-five."

A smile from him at last. "Sweetheart, I rest my case."

She too, smiled.

By eleven they were in her kitchen and he was still not ready to let go of Selena's planned living arrangements. He was unable to relax.

Even in sleep his muscles were tight and angry. Hours before dawn colored the sky, he left the bed and moved to the window, staring into the night.

Heleena sat up, but remained in bed, holding back.

He must have won the war that raged within him, because when he rejoined her, there was a calm resolve about him.

"For once, I can hear you thinking." She teased.

"Then I must sound ridiculous. Here I am admonishing my daughter about her life style and I'm living a lie everyday of my own life."

They were sitting side by side, their backs supported by pillows.

"Why does it take us so long to realize the future comes minute by minute? That it isn't some place we go to and when we get there, we can put things right and correct every mistake we ever made."

He'd crossed into another realm and it was his own mistakes plaguing him now. She slipped into his arms. Al had discovered his future. She didn't dare dwell beyond the here and now. These arms are real.

"You will work through this, just as you work through everything else."

"I have. But, I'm annoyed with myself for wasting all the time I could have had with you. I made a mistake and much of that time has slipped away."

"Contrary to all the books and talk shows, that say we're in charge of our own destinies, the truth of the matter is, outside events often irrevocably alter the course of our lives."

* * *

Heleena stayed with Karen until after midnight. They'd sorted through piles of clothes and shoes. Karen decided to take only enough clothes to fill four pieces of luggage. She'd boxed the remaining clothes she wanted to keep. Scooter would ship those to her in Memphis once she found her own place. Everything else was to be given away.

There were a few pieces of furniture she wanted, the lime-print love seat and matching chairs from the rec-room and Judy's bedroom furniture for her own use. Whatever was left in the house, she told Scooter to dispose of as he saw fit.

They'd done more talking than packing. To her surprise, Heleena found, as they chatted, she actually envied Karen's decision to chuck much of the present and start over.

"I didn't think you had the courage."

"It didn't take courage. Once I started to think about my life, the decision was easy."

Heleena waited for her to continue.

"What happened with Judy gave me time to think about things. In my mind I have been through every minute of my life since I came to D.C. You can't imagine, day after day, recalling forgotten incidents and remembering people I haven't seen in years. Things my aunts talked about. But, try as I might, I can't remember enough of my baby's little-girl days."

She sat on the bed, staring at some inner place and continued. "There are holes I can't fill. Even with Scooter. I realized that at some point we stopped connecting. Maybe from a distance I can make sense of this mess. I certainly can't do it here."

"What about Scooter?'

"What do you mean?"

"This is a tough time for him too. He'll be alone here."

"He needs to find his peace too. We haven't talked much in the last couple of months and things don't look good for us. You, of all people, should understand."

"Leaving the man who couldn't love you more?" From her perch on the bed Heleena looked for some clue to explain why her friend was walking away from the man who cherished her so.

"He needs time too."

Since the day Karen announced she was going back to Memphis, Heleena tried to change her mind. Her arguments only made Karen more set in her resolve.

This new Karen was making decisions that had nothing to do with money or what people might think about her actions. She was going forward with nothing but a strong desire to find the true Karen.

Even though she disagreed with this decision, Heleena found it exciting, another chance to start over.

"If there is anything around here you'd like to have take it."

"I don't think so. But I know Marva would like to have that sculptured iron teapot you bought in Bermuda."

"I'll put it in a box and Scooter will see that she gets it. When is she coming home?"

"I don't know. One thing's for sure, she is not going back to the D.C. Government. She sent in her letter of resignation two weeks ago."

"Well, well, she finally made up her mind. She's hated that job for years. What will she do now, stay at home?"

"I can't see her doing that."

"Too bad she didn't leave before now. She might have been able to recapture Al's attention."

Her back was to Heleena, making it impossible to see her facial expression. But, she went on, "I think she must have thrown in the towel or she's got her eyes on someone else."

Even so, Heleena masked her discomfort by walking to the bureau drawers and lifting out the remaining contents.

"Did Al say when she was coming home?"

"No."

"That's odd he didn't tell you."

Into the night, they'd talked about everybody in their circle, those who had passed through their lives and meaningless events from bygone days. Now as she readied herself to take her friend to the airport and say goodbye, for a time anyway, she dressed slower than usual. She deliberately selected a special pantsuit. It was important for her to look her best on this day. Karen was taking a major step and she wanted to radiate confidence in her decision.

Cooler weather had finally arrived. Maybe to stay. On this bright October morning, the promise of a glorious fall was evident. The brilliant reds and yellows she loved so much had begun to appear.

My favorite time of the year.

What should have been a golden day for her was instead tinged with anxiety and a sense of loss. The years had slipped by so quickly. The pace of their passing unnoticed and unappreciated. She didn't know how she would make it through the coming days without Karen and possibly without Marva.

As she drove through the cool morning her thoughts were running in all directions, lighting on images of events that were no more. Her life, like the lives of her friends, had changed so desperately, during the last five months, she could no longer predict where she was headed and this feeling unsettled her.

To calm herself she replayed the conversation she'd had with Al Tuesday evening. Emotions were sweeping through him like a storm.

She'd gone straight to his office from work. They were spending more time together. Lately, he'd begun to recall advice his mother had given him as he, too, tried to sort through the changes in his life.

"She knew me well," he said. "Trying to be a man just across the river from hell was not going to be easy. And she said it was her duty to caution me--life is like walking down a quiet country road. You can see in three directions, straight ahead and out of the corner of each eye. No matter where you turn you can only see in three directions. Even being on the lookout constantly, at some time in your life somebody is going to come up behind you, without your knowing and that person will be in a position to cause you grief.

But don't be hard on yourself when it happens, she'd said. Just protect yourself the best you can."

"While I was busy protecting myself from Charlie's heavy yoke, I wasn't quick enough to avoid a lighter, but just as heavy one."

His fear that Selena would make the same mistake was justified in his eyes.

* * *

209

Having arrived at Karen's two hours earlier than she'd promised, Heleena was surprised to see she was ready to leave. The luggage set in the foyer."You take more than this when you go on weekend trips."

"Even if I wanted to take more, I won't have space for most of what fills my closets."

"Why not put the things you're not sure about in storage?"

"I'm taking a big step Heleena, please don't make it harder for me. I have closed myself off from the heartaches I feel everyday here in this house. I want new things around me now, in a new place."

There was no need arguing with her. "Okay. Where's Scooter?"

"We said our good-byes earlier."

"I can't believe you're really walking out on him."

"How many times do I have to say this so you will understand? I need to be away now--to be by myself."

"Going back to your mother's house doesn't sound as if you want to be alone."

"That's only a temporary arrangement. As soon as I find a place, I'll be out of there. The only reason I'm staying at her house instead of my sister's is, I don't want to listen to all the bullshit and answer endless questions."

Heleena's laugh caused Karen to turn and look at her with a question in her eyes.

"You said it, I didn't."

Heleena wasn't ready to let go of Karen's decisions about her marriage. "You're not planning to file for divorce are you?"

"No."

She was relieved. All these swift changes were beginning to strain her ability to cope.

* * *

They were slowed by traffic as they headed for National. Out of the blue Karen asked her, "When you think about Greg, what are your thoughts? How do you remember your time with him? Was there ever a time you would take him back?"

Minutes passed before she answered.

"No, and no and no again. I'm not the same woman who drifted into marriage with him."

"That sure is a strange way of describing your marriage."

"Well, it's hard for me to provide a more accurate description of our life together. I never felt comfortable, secure and emotionally intimate with him."

"Go on," Karen urged her when she hesitated.

"For lack of a better term, I must use the word love, I never really loved him the way a woman should love her husband and I don't think he felt that way about me either."

"This is deep."

"In my way of thinking, your feeling for a man is magical, powerful. It's like a beautiful flower floating on a breeze. You grab hold as it floats by. And if you're lucky enough to do all the right things, you'll preserve its beauty. But, if you open your hand and it's sucked away; love, like the flower, is gone forever. You can never get that love again. Greg and I didn't have that kind of love."

"But the two of you got along together."

"We settled, like a lot of people back then."

"Who do you know fits this kind of love?"

"That is exactly how Scooter loves you."

"Maybe. But, for so many couples, their time has passed."

"Not if they still share a spark of whatever feelings drew them together. It has to be more than a new baby, new home, new job or town."

"You've given much thought to this."

"Do you understand what I'm saying?"

"I think so."

"Just don't shut Scooter out of your life. You will never get another man like him."

"Excuse me?"

"We are not young anymore and eligible men our age are scarce. Look at me; you don't see any men beating down my door. They're just not out here. So you'd better keep the man you have."

Karen took a long incredulous look at her.

* * *

Once Karen checked in, they sat in the open gallery talking quietly, enjoying their final hours together, Heleena doing most of the talking. Karen was more subdued. Finally, she said what was on her mind.

"I didn't say anything yesterday because I didn't want to spoil our last day together. But, I feel I must warn you. Be careful with Al, he can break your heart."

Heleena stared, rigid with shock. The calm she desperately maintained during these parting days shattered. The surprised look on her face brought a smile from Karen.

"Oh yes, I know what's going on between you two."

Heleena's pulse beat wildly. "What do you mean?"

"Okay you want me to spell it out? This thing you have going with him. And, Scooter knows, too."

Still Heleena kept silent.

Karen pressed on. "You were in such turmoil at the beginning of the summer, kind of desperate like."

"Thanks."

"We all noticed you. Then, your whole demeanor changed. You even blossomed like a woman involved. All of a sudden you were more relaxed, self-satisfied. Think about it. The only men you were around consistently were Scooter and Al. But, the nail in the coffin came the night I called you at three o'clock in the morning, when we found my baby. As hysterical as I was, I realized there was someone else in your bed--and who was that, our man Prince."

Heleena was speechless.

"Everybody thinks I don't pay attention to the people around me, but that isn't so. I began to watch you and Al, something to do, to take my mind off my own situation."

"Oh boy."

"As far as I can tell, you may be the only thing he has ever wanted and did not have, until now. You are in a dangerous situation, Heleena. Just be careful."

* * *

When Karen's flight was announced she turned to Heleena and smiled. But there was deep sadness lurking in her eyes. She was going home to lick her wounds as much as to start again.

They'd been like sisters for more than twenty-five years--sharing all of their adult lives. Every single day. Fleetingly, she remembered that hot sweaty night so long ago when they first met.

Heleena hugged her tightly, then let go. When her friend walked through the gate, she carried with her a bright period of time, an era forever encapsulated in a special corner of her heart.

www.ingramcontent.com/pod-product-compliance
Lightning Source LLC
Chambersburg PA
CBHW030313290526
45785CB00001B/339